Banish Anxiety

Banish Anxiety
How to stop worrying and take charge of your life

Dr Kenneth Hambly

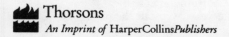
Thorsons
An Imprint of HarperCollins*Publishers*

Dedicated to my wife Alison

Thorsons
An Imprint of HarperCollins*Publishers*
77–85 Fulham Palace Road,
Hammersmith, London W6 8JB

Published by Thorsons 1991
10 9 8 7 6 5 4 3 2

A catalogue record for this book
is available from the British Library

ISBN 0 7225 2227 4

Printed and bound in Great Britain by
Mackays of Chatham PLC, Chatham, Kent

Contents

Introduction

Everyone feels anxious from time to time. Anxiety is natural and normal in many situations. You will feel anxious before an interview for a new job, or before you have to make a speech. You will certainly feel anxious if you have to face danger. Everyone reacts to these difficult situations by feeling anxious, and that feeling is understandable and acceptable even if we don't particularly enjoy it. So what's the problem?

The problem for many people is that they feel anxious all the time, even when there is no reason to feel that way. Other people may experience excessive anxiety in some difficult situations and so they don't manage those situations very well, and then there are people who feel anxious in situations which other people might think are completely routine and non-threatening. For all of these people anxiety is a problem.

Anxiety is only a problem if it limits your life, or if it makes your life less enjoyable than it might otherwise be. Anxiety is a problem if you think it is a problem, no matter what other people might say or think. Other people don't know what you may have to go through. Other people may well not understand how you feel, or the very unpleasant sensations you experience.

If anxiety is a problem for you it need not be. You don't have to be anxious. You can banish anxiety. It isn't easy, but if you go about it the right way it can be done, and you can do it. This book will tell you how to go about banishing anxiety from your life.

Chapter 1

Anxiety — what is it?

If you suffer from excessive anxiety you probably feel that you know all that there is to know about it. You will certainly know a great deal, and you will know how unpleasant, or even disabling, it can be. But what is anxiety, and what is excessive anxiety, and what is an anxiety state?

The first thing to realize is that there is only one kind of anxiety. The anxiety you feel in certain situations is exactly the same anxiety that anyone would feel if they were faced with real physical danger. The driver of the runaway train will feel a little understandable anxiety when he realizes that his life is in danger. Fortunately we aren't faced with physical danger too often, but everyone does experience anxiety from time to time.

That anxiety may occur before we go on stage at an amateur theatrical event, or before an interview. It is the same sensation of anxiety we would experience if we were facing physical danger even though we know that our lives aren't threatened. Danger comes in different forms. No one is immune to anxiety.

The second thing to realize about anxiety is that it has a mental component and a physical component. Anxiety isn't just an emotion, it is also a set of symptoms or sensations, and indeed it may be that these physical sensations exist even when we don't feel mentally anxious. Sometimes it is these physical symptoms which bring someone to his or her doctor. The symptoms may exist without any awareness of anxiety, almost as if the person. was suffering from a physical illness. That may seem a little strange, but it is a common occurrence. One survey showed that thirteen people out of every hundred experience the symptoms of anxiety to a degree which affects their everyday lives, and that is one definition of an anxiety state.

We all experience anxiety from time to time, but when the unpleasant symptoms affect our everyday lives we can be said to have an anxiety state, and then we have a problem.

Anxiety states and phobias — what are they?

As a family doctor I see many people who suffer from the symptoms of excessive anxiety. Over the years I have taken a special interest in anxiety, and made a study of it. Excessive anxiety can afflict people of any age, of any occupation or social class, and of either sex. People afflicted with it are confused and often frightened by the strength of the symptoms they experience. They wonder just what's happening to them.

I have treated many people who have been suffering from excessive anxiety, from an anxiety state or a phobia. In all of these conditions, the individual experiences the symptoms of anxiety to a degree which he or she finds unacceptable. They have all been disturbed, troubled or even frightened by their symptoms. Often they have felt lonely and misunderstood, and always they have felt helpless. They have wondered if there was any solution to their problem, and in every case there *has* been a solution. Banishing anxiety is quite possible if you go about it the right way.

One patient, Michael, was a senior civil servant with years of experience at the highest level of his profession, but he was respected locally for a quite different reason. Despite his advancing years he was an excellent village cricketer. He was at his happiest whilst playing cricket, but his success was his undoing. He was made captain of the team in its centenary year. It was a great honour, but that honour brought problems for Michael.

The truth was that although Michael was a senior civil servant, he had problems with public speaking. He could manage very well in his own environment in the civil service, but he dreaded the thought of having to make speeches and present prizes at cricket club functions. When he told me about it I was very surprised. Like everyone else I would never have guessed that Michael, whom I knew very well, had a problem with excessive anxiety.

Another patient who consulted me was Sarah. Again she was

someone I knew well as she had three children under ten, and like most families they had their share of childhood illnesses about which she would consult me. Sarah was a likeable, outgoing young woman who was apparently very competent and able. She lived in a council house and was happily married. One day she came to the surgery and before she could say anything she burst into tears. She simply sat in the chair weeping, unable to speak. When she had settled down she told me what was wrong.

It seemed that she was almost housebound by a condition she just couldn't understand. It had come on over the past few months. It seemed that every time she went out of the house she began to feel uneasy and frightened. Her feelings were worse in the supermarket, and became unbearable in the queue at the check-out where she sometimes thought she was going to die. She had no idea why she felt so bad, and she had no idea what to do about it. She had now almost stopped going out. To her, life hardly seemed to be worth living.

Then there was Jean. Her anxiety took the form of a dog phobia. She liked dogs well enough, but they frightened her. It wasn't just big dogs which did this. Any dog, even a Pekinese, made her very uncomfortable. If she had to visit a house where the owner had a dog she had to telephone in advance and ask that the dog be locked away. If she met a dog in the street she froze, and now she would travel miles to avoid any contact with a dog. As dogs abound in the streets, her life was becoming increasingly difficult.

All of these people suffered from the symptoms of anxiety. The symptoms they experienced were exactly the same. Michael experienced them when he was required to speak in public. Sarah had them in the supermarket, and Jean experienced them anywhere where there was a dog. The symptoms were the same for each of them, and they could experience the same symptoms if they even thought about the situations they found difficult. They had one other thing in common, each thinking that they were the only ones to suffer these symptoms, and they all felt embarrassed and about the way they felt.

If you feel anxious much of the time you may not have thought of your anxiety in terms of a list of physical symptoms. You may just have noticed that you feel anxious. Conversely, you may have been aware of headaches or a shaky hand without knowing why, without even feeling anxious. If all this sounds a little confusing don't worry. Anxiety is anxiety, a human condition with a mental and a physical side which is extremely common—and extremely treatable.

Why be afraid?

The actual symptoms these three people experienced were exactly the ones they would have experienced if they had been faced by a charging bull. The body's reaction to physical stress is exactly the same as its reaction to psychological stress, and it isn't very pleasant. Worse than that, it can be very limiting. It can spoil your entire life.

None of these people thought that they would come to any harm from the situations which produced their anxiety. Michael knew that he wouldn't die making a speech. Sarah didn't really think that she would die at the check-out, and Jean wasn't frightened of being bitten by a dog, just of the idea of a dog. If they didn't fear physical danger, then what were they afraid of?

The intense sensations they felt in difficult situations were real, and they were frightening. Jean wasn't afraid of dogs at all. She liked dogs. She would have liked to have had a dog of her own. What she feared was the symptoms which dogs produced in her, and these symptoms were just as real and even more immediate than they would have been if she had had a dreadful overpowering allergy to dogs. That fear of her symptoms was completely understandable.

No one would be in the least surprised if you were afraid of a charging bull. You would be unwise not to be. It seems less reasonable to be scared of a dog, or of a supermarket queue. It is, however, quite understandable to be scared of the intense sensations which you experience in such a situation if you have excessive anxiety. What we have to ask ourselves is not why we are scared of our symptoms, which is reasonable and under-standable, but rather why we get the symptoms in the first place.

So we're not going to use the word fear any more, or talk about being scared. It isn't appropriate. People who experience excessive anxiety are almost always very courageous, and as we will see, any fear they experience is fear of their symptoms, not fear of a situation. There is all the difference in the world between the two. Anxiety is a terrible handicap, a burden which has to be carried through every waking hour. Dealing with it, leading a reasonably normal life, looking after a family or holding down a job takes massive effort and courage. You know how much courage that it takes if you have experienced anxiety. You also know how lonely it can be, because those people, even those close to us, who have not experienced anxiety do not know, and cannot know, just how bad it can be.

Is anxiety a new condition? Why have I never heard about it?

Why is being anxious so frightening? Why do you know so little about it? Why do you feel that you are the only one to suffer, and that no one else can understand? There seems to be a conspiracy of silence about anxiety, and you feel you are one of its victims.

Nonsense! You are not the only one to suffer from anxiety. Many, many people experience anxiety and there have always been people who were anxious, but there may be a conspiracy of silence. People tend not to talk about their problems in case they are misunderstood. Like all psychological difficulties there is still a stigma attached to anxiety.

People who suffer from anxiety feel that they will be less likely to be promoted at work, or that they may be shunned by friends who don't understand or who don't want to understand. Indeed, even in this age when anxiety and similar problems are beginning to be talked about and written about in magazines, much of this is still true. You will have learned from your own experience that anxiety is a taboo topic. This may well be because many people feel threatened themselves if the subject is raised. They just don't want to know. It is easy to feel alone. People just don't talk about it.

In days gone by the condition was talked about in terms of having the 'vapours' or feeling liverish, and people suffering from these may well have had what we would now term an anxiety state. There was a different language used for discussing illness, a different concept of illness and different fashions. Scientific medicine is arguably new to the twentieth century. Remember that medicine used to be an art! In the days of Jane Austen, having the vapours was quite socially acceptable amongst the middle and upper classes. Having an anxiety state nowadays is somehow less acceptable, and that can make the sufferer feel socially inadequate.

Many famous people have had anxiety states. Florence Nightingale may have had agoraphobia, an extreme form of phobic anxiety. Charles Darwin certainly suffered from excessive anxiety. So I'm quite sure that excessive anxiety isn't a new condition. You aren't the first person to suffer from it and you won't be the last.

Anxiety was first seriously studied as long ago as the 1920s when a great deal was written about it. Many of the techniques outlined in this book and commonly used to treat anxiety were invented then, and subsequently neglected.

Today many people in the public eye suffer from anxiety, though few will admit to it. The late Harold Macmillan, the most urbane of British Prime Ministers, used to be very anxious before he had to make a speech, even if it was only a speech at his old preparatory school prize giving. A friend of mine was sitting on the platform beside a previous Prime Minister at a conference when she noticed that he was shaking so much that his chair was rattling. Michael, the cricketing civil servant who was anxious about public speaking, might take comfort from that knowledge.

Even actors aren't immune. Some are physically sick before a performance or a television appearance. I knew one who had severe stomach pains from a supposed ulcer before every performance. Anxiety is all around us.

How serious is my anxiety?

You are the only one who knows how much your anxiety interferes with your everyday life. Some feelings of anxiety in some situations have to be considered to be normal. Everyone suffers from anxiety, and it is a natural phenomenon which has a real purpose in nature.

In your case it may be different. It may be that your feelings of anxiety limit your life. You may have a phobia about, say, lifts, so that you have to walk up four flights of stairs every day instead of taking the lift like everyone else.

You may not like crowds, and so you may avoid crowds and that may include concerts and all the public events you would love to attend. You could be anxious about anything, and that includes sex and similar very personal and private parts of your life. Or you may just feel worried and uneasy all of the time without knowing why. If any of these things interfere with your life in any form, then it is serious, and you should take it seriously.

How do I know my problem is anxiety?

If you're reading this book you must have at least a suspicion that you are suffering from excessive anxiety. Most people know what their problem is, but there is no way of proving it. It is however, possible to exclude other medical reasons for the way you feel. The main medical condition which mimics an anxiety state is an overactive thyroid gland, and your doctor will be able to do a blood test to clarify the situation.

Your own diagnosis of excessive anxiety can usually be made with confidence because you are familiar with the sensations you get when you have 'normal' anxiety, such as before an interview. Anxiety is just anxiety no matter how or when it is produced, and when you've got it you know. It isn't quite so straightforward if you are experiencing the long-term symptoms of anxiety without the acute feelings. You might have tension headaches or excessive tiredness without, say, the tummy churnings. You might wonder if you are physically ill. In that case your doctor will help you, but every anxious person has some of the symptoms and almost everyone can make the diagnosis themselves. This book will help you.

Knowing you have anxiety and accepting that your anxiety can produce physical symptoms is another thing altogether. Yet it should be fairly obvious. Everyone has had a churning tummy or diarrhoea before a stressful event. We have all had a shaky hand and a dry mouth before speaking in public. If anxiety becomes an everyday, all day, experience, surely it must produce symptoms all of the time, and surely those symptoms will be worse in stressful situations. As muscle tension is the most common result of chronic anxiety, fatigue and muscle pains are the most common complaints.

Some people find this hard to accept. They feel that the suggestion that they have a psychological condition is inappropriate or insulting, and seek physical explanations for their symptoms. One man I knew insisted that he had malaria, despite evidence to the contrary. Another thought he had rheumatism, and many people now believe that they have, or have had, a virus illness which accounts for the way they feel.

Everyone must manage their lives in the best way they can, but if you can accept that you are suffering from symptoms produced by excessive anxiety rather than an obscure physical illness, you are lucky. In the first place you have faced up to the real cause of your symptoms, and in the second place anxiety can be cured. It isn't possible to rid yourself of an illness you don't have. Coming to terms with the real reasons for your condition, and perhaps buying this book, is the first and most important step along the road to banishing your anxiety. You are already winning.

A word to the young

I have said that anxiety can afflict anyone at any age. That means people in their teens too, and that is an age when you need all of your confidence, and when you really don't need to be anxious. You have your entire life ahead of you. You have jobs to get, interviews to attend, dates to go on. None of this is easy under normal circumstances. Excessive anxiety makes it much more difficult. Still, you can beat it, and all that is said in this book applies to you.

So what now?

You have started by beginning to understand. The more we understand the more obvious are the methods which we must use if we are to banish our anxiety. It's all straightforward, but it isn't easy. We will take it one step at a time and we will win. Something which is at the moment mysterious and disturbing will be revealed as a common, logical and completely understandable phenomenon, an everyday matter which can be dealt with in a surprisingly everyday manner.

Understanding our anxiety means understanding something about ourselves, and something about how our bodies work. It can and should be enjoyable, and I hope that this book will be your guide. I would also like it to be a friend, because I know how lonely anxiety can make you, and how isolated you can become. You aren't alone, you are one of many, and the three people whose problems I mentioned earlier also felt alone and unhappy. They overcame their anxiety. So can you.

REMEMBER:

- Anxiety is a normal phenomenon.
- There is only one kind of anxiety, however it is caused.
- Anxiety has a mental and a physical side.
- Anxiety states are common.
- Excessive anxiety *can* be banished.

Chapter 2

Anxiety—a learned condition

Some people suffer from increased anxiety all of the time. These people are in a minority because most sufferers find that their anxiety is worse in certain stressful situations.

If you are one of the people who feel more anxious in some situations than in others, you will feel sweaty, your heart will race and you will feel panicky in these specific situations. These physical sensations can be so overwhelming that you may even avoid these difficult situations if you possibly can and in this way anxiety can change your life. It can limit what you do—even what jobs you can take.

It can all seem very frightening, confusing and totally inexplicable. You may feel very isolated, very much alone and misunderstood. It can lead you to despair. It may make no sense to you at all. I know that you are anxious to get on with the business of treating your excessive anxiety, but if you are an anxious person it is worth while taking the time now to really understand what is happening to you and why. That is the first part of your cure, so let's take one step at a time and begin by looking at anxiety in some detail.

Anxiety is a natural phenomenon

Anxiety is common to all animals. It is essential to their survival and there is nothing strange about it. So why does it seem so baffling when we experience it to excess? It is after all, a purely natural phenomenon.

Let's go back to the beginning. Let's look at anxiety in the animal world. Think of a grazing animal on one of the great plains of Africa. The main problem for a grazing animal is that it might one day be eaten by a lion. It spends most of its life grazing quietly, but every now and then a lion may appear. The lion may just be out for a walk, but on the other hand it may be hungry, and it may be hunting. If it is the grazing animal is in trouble and has to be ready to run for its life—literally.

Fortunately nature has equipped the animal for just this emergency. It keeps the lion in sight. It has learned that the lion means danger. Its life depends on its body's ability to get out of that danger. If the lion charges the animal will have to run, as fast, as far and for as long as it has ever run in its life before. It will need almost supernatural powers, and it will get them.

Let us assume that the lion charges. Without hesitation, without making any decisions, the grazing animal runs, and automatically certain things happen to its body. This is a purely automatic, conditioned response and it is vitally important to survival. A powerful substance called adrenalin is released into the bloodstream.

The release of this substance allows an immediate response in many organs. Muscles tighten, blood is diverted to them and sugar is pumped into that blood from the liver so that they can work harder. Breathing is deeper and there is more oxygen in the blood.

This amazing reaction has always been called the 'flight or fight' reaction. It tones our bodies up so that we can run away faster than we normally could, or stand and fight with more strength than we would normally have. All mammals have it, and so humans have it too.

Our ancestors depended on the 'flight or fight' reaction for their survival. They depended on it when they were outrunning predators, or when they were hunting, involved in the thrill of the chase. In our own time, if you were walking across a field and encountered an angry bull, your life would depend on it too. You would run faster and further than you ever thought you would be able to. You have heard people in this sort of emergency situation say: 'I don't know where I got the strength from.' Now you know—it was the adrenalin in their bloodstream.

This 'flight or fight' reaction is automatic. It switches on all by itself, and it switches off by itself. It is your body's automatic response to danger, but how does your body know what is dangerous? How does this vital reaction switch on? The answer is that it is a learned response. We learn what is dangerous from our parents, from our environment and most of all from our experience. We learn all our lives, just like the grazing animal on the Serengeti.

The split second we see danger, hear danger or feel danger the reaction switches on. We don't have to do anything consciously at all. It is an instantaneous, 'all systems go' reaction which allows us to respond to the dangers in our environment, but that's all very well when our bodies have learned the right lessons. What happens if we have learned the wrong lessons? What happens if over the years our bodies have learned that some things are dangerous which other people might not think were dangerous at all? Obviously the reaction will switch on at inappropriate times and in inappropriate situations.

Animals do this. Everyone knows a dog which runs and hides when there's a storm. It may well be having an adrenalin-type reaction as a result of hearing the thunder crack. It isn't in physical danger, but its perception is that there is danger because it has learned the wrong lesson. Horses, which are grazing animals in the wild dependent on quick reflex reactions, may shy away from something like a plastic bag in the hedge because they wrongly associate it with danger. They will always shy at a plastic bag because the reaction is programmed in, because the horse has learned the wrong lesson. Moreover, if a horse gets a fright, it will remember that place and it will react every time it goes there. For the horse, that particular place is dangerous, and when the horse recognizes it it will produce adrenalin and have the familiar adrenalin-type reaction.

Humans have an added difficulty. We can think in more complex ways. We also have a different concept of danger. For you and me, making a speech might become a dangerous situation, and because we can think ahead, the very thought of having to make that speech next week can induce the adrenalin reaction.

Some people, and some animals, are more nervous than others. The flight or fight reaction turns on more easily and more often. Animal experiments have shown that if an animal is stressed it produces more adrenalin and so it is more prone to anxiety, so that if you or I are of a naturally nervous disposition, or if we are stressed, these learned reactions occur more often and may become intrusive, and we develop the symptoms of anxiety.

That brings us up to date. Those powerful and seemingly inexplicable sensations which an anxious person experiences in some situations are in fact easily explained. They are a natural phenomenon in the natural world, nothing to do with going mad or being unable to cope, and only partly to do with the stresses of modern life. What that person experiences is simply an exaggeration of a reaction everyone experiences, a reaction which all animals also experience. It is nothing to be frightened of, and as it is a 'learned' reaction it can be 'unlearned' if you go about it the right way.

What is a phobia?

A phobia is simply the experience of the sensations associated with anxiety related to a particular situation or perhaps to an animal or even an inanimate object. People can be phobic about spiders, lifts, heights, crowds, aeroplanes, hens, dogs and cats—anything. If you asked a roomful of people if those with a phobia would raise their hands, just about everyone present would because phobias are very common. Not everyone with a phobia is over-anxious. It can be an isolated problem, but most people who are over-anxious have a phobic element to their anxiety state. It is worse in certain situations and it will always be triggered in those situations.

Phobias develop in the way I have described. It is usually triggered by an unpleasant, sometimes forgotten experience and this experience starts the phobia. Its function in the animal world and in our own primitive past is clear, it is the old 'flight or fight' reaction, a reaction to something perceived to be dangerous. A phobia is thus nothing like as bizarre a phenomenon as it first appears.

For some reason, no doubt because phobias are so common, people who suffer from them usually freely admit the fact and may treat it as a joke. People think that they understand phobias, whereas people with excessive anxiety tend to see their problem as being something that they should be ashamed of, and you won't find many people admitting to having an anxiety state.

Yet an anxiety state, which is also a condition where excessive anxiety is felt in certain situations, is almost the same as a phobia. The main difference is that with an anxiety state the feeling of anxiety is experienced more often, and in more situations than a phobia. It may be that an anxiety state is seen as being more disabling, more threatening to a job or to relationships, but it is also true that people with anxiety states are frightened and confused by them, and they find that others are less understanding.

Someone with a phobia is one of a crowd. Someone with an anxiety state is on his own. At least that's how it can feel.

How does excessive anxiety happen?

If anxiety is such a normal phenomenon, such an important part of the natural world, how can it be so distressing to the individual? How can it change and limit your life? The answer has to be that natural phenomena are useful in their proper place. There is a proper place for the adrenalin 'flight or fight' reaction, and that is when it occurs in response to danger, particularly if that danger is physical and short-lived. We aren't expected to run away forever, after all.

If we are exposed to low-key, constant danger, something that is ever present, there when we wake and there when we go to bed, the situation is very different. The danger doesn't have to be physical because to our bodies, danger is danger no matter how it is caused, and a mental threat is as real as a physical one. In this new situation adrenalin is still produced, but now it is produced in a small amount all of the time. This is not what nature intended.

If we make no physical response to this stress, the effects of the adrenalin become very unpleasant, frightening and sometimes painful. If we were running away we wouldn't be aware of these sensations as they would just be part of our body's physical response. Now they cease to be beneficial, and can become a distinct liability.

Some people can use these sensations to their own advantage. Many performers feel the need for some tension before going on stage if they are to give their best and the same is true of athletes. Getting the adrenalin going is one reason for the pre-match team talk, and some tennis players will create an atmosphere of tension during a match to deliberately increase their adrenalin output and improve their performance. Even so, performers and athletes know that the right amount of adrenalin helps performance, too much spoils it.

That is what has gone wrong for you. You are producing too much of this perfectly natural substance adrenalin, and producing it in the wrong situations. Adrenalin is a substance which has powerful actions on many of the body's functions. It is released into the bloodstream by the adrenal glands, situated just above the kidney, and its release is triggered by complex factors, the most important of which is exposure to danger or stress.

How does an anxiety state develop?

You have learned how to be anxious. It's as easy as that. Well, almost as easy. Your excessive anxiety has just crept up on you, but that is because your body has been learning how to be anxious, perhaps for years. Of course you haven't been aware of that, but then there are many things that happen to your body of which you aren't aware. It's fair to say that you are completely unaware of most of the things which happen to your body because they work automatically.

You don't have to focus your eyes, or adjust them for night vision. You don't have to produce saliva—that happens when you see or smell food. You don't have to make your intestine contract in waves so that your food passes through your body, and when you stand up your blood-pressure is adjusted automatically, and the tone in your muscles is readjusted. Adrenalin is also produced automatically. You can't control any of these functions. There is no way that you can control your blood-pressure or stop the production of saliva, and sadly there is no way that you can directly control the output of adrenalin from the adrenal glands. There is a reason for that, as there is a reason for everything that happens to our bodies. The production of adrenalin is a natural function. We need adrenalin. When we need it we need it quickly. Its production is physiological, or normal, a natural immediate response to stress and danger. In the right amounts it is vital but too much is destructive.

Is over-anxiety an illness?

This depends how you define an illness. If having too little insulin is an illness, maybe having too much adrenalin is an illness. Certainly it can be seen to be a disease, as any sufferer will know. In the international classification of diseases, there is an entry for anxiety states. So let's call it a disease; a disease which can be cured.

All that has happened is that the adrenal glands have learned over a long period of time to produce too much adrenalin. The 'control' has come to be set a little too high. Re-educate your body to turn down that control, to produce less adrenalin and the problem is solved. Easy? Well, not quite. It isn't easy to re-educate your body. It takes time, commitment and effort, and you must go about it the right way.

Why haven't I been able to cure myself?

You have been fighting your anxiety state ever since you started to feel unwell. You may well have been making heroic efforts to control the way you feel, doing everything you can. Most people with excessive anxiety do just that. They hate their anxiety, the thing which holds them back and prevents them from leading a normal life.

It is difficult to rid yourself of anxiety simply because it is an exaggeration of a normal state and you can't control your body at will. You can't for example slow down your intestinal contractions, because they are automatic, but some people, such as Indian mystics, can control some of their body's functions. They may be able to control the sensation of pain, and can thus push needles through their flesh. That is a convincing, if distressing, example of what can be done if you go about controlling your body in the right way.

We can't all be Indian mystics, but we can all learn to control some functions of our bodies. I don't mean by hypnosis, meditation or yoga; I mean by much more mundane and ordinary methods: by understanding our bodies and our problems and by the daily practice of relaxation. It is possible by these simple means to reverse the learning process which has been causing our anxiety, to turn it round and begin to learn how to be relaxed and comfortable. We can put adrenalin back in its box, ready to be used when it is needed.

How do i make a start?

In order to start reading this book you must have had some idea that the physical symptoms you were experiencing were due to anxiety, or stress, or something like that. Many people can't understand that concept. They can't see how physical symptoms can be due to a state of anxiety. They know that they are ill, but they are sure that the illness from which they are suffering is a purely physical illness. You have worked out for yourself that you are suffering from excessive anxiety, and so you are already streets ahead of many people who suffer from that distressing condition.

Now that you have read this far I hope that you will see the logic behind that concept, how straightforward it is. I hope that much of the anguish, uncertainty and worry has disappeared now that you know that anxiety is a normal and necessary part of nature. Dull, lethargic animals don't do too well in nature. We need adrenalin. It is the spice of life, the thing which takes people to horror movies and up in roller-coasters. It is excitement. You may have too much of it, but that isn't the end of the world.

You know that excessive anxiety can be banished, and you know how. In the rest of this book we will get down to the details.

How long will it take?

This depends on many things. It will take a long time to disappear completely, but it should improve quite rapidly. You should soon start to feel better about your anxiety. You always feel better about something you understand, and you will feel much better and much more confident when you start to treat your anxiety.

No matter how bad your anxiety is, no matter how long you have had it, it *can* be banished. That is a certainty. That doesn't mean that you can become a television newsreader overnight. You will have the same anxieties and stresses as others, perhaps even more than some others, but you will be able to control them, and you will be able to lead an ordinary life. We can ask for no more.

REMEMBER:

- Anxiety is often felt in difficult situations.
- The sensations of anxiety are produced by adrenalin.
- Adrenalin is a natural substance. All animals need it.
- The adrenalin reaction is learned; therefore, we can teach our bodies to produce less adrenalin.

Chapter 3

Anxiety—a mental and a physical condition

Excessive anxiety is indeed a miserable condition. It is frightening and confusing and it can drive you to despair. It fills your entire day. You wake up with it, and it is there when you go to bed at night. It is hard to think about it rationally, no matter how carefully it has been explained and how hard you try. That may be because it is a physical presence, a great weight painfully balanced on your shoulders, something which is oppressive and all-pervasive.

Yet you have to make sense out of it. At the moment it may still feel like an amorphous mass, something ill-defined and obscure; but if you are to banish your anxiety you have to have a clear idea just what it is you are trying to banish. But if you don't have a clear idea of just what anxiety really is, and that isn't surprising because it's a difficult thing to define, how can you develop a plan for dealing with it?

Anxiety, a psychological or a physical condition?

So just what is anxiety in our modern world? We know how it works in nature, and in emergency situations, but when we look at it in the context of our everyday lives it can still be confusing. Is it a state of mind? A friend of mine is a very anxious person, by which I mean that she worries a lot about all sorts of things. Is a worrier just someone who has too much adrenalin in the circulation, or is a worrier someone who lives a reasonably normal contented life but who happens to have an anxious type of personality? We use the word anxiety loosely in all sorts of different ways. You may be anxious to get on with this book, hoping that you will soon learn how to control your own anxiety. It can be very confusing.

Let's nail anxiety down. We can begin by deciding what it isn't. We aren't just talking about someone who has an anxious personality, someone who may have difficulty making decisions, someone who worries. We aren't talking about someone who always thinks and fears the worst. It's possible to be morbid and miserable just because that's the way you are made, and it doesn't follow that you are suffering from excessive anxiety in the form of an anxiety state.

People who worry can also have an anxiety state of course, but many people who suffer from the symptoms of anxiety to a degree which affects their everyday lives are just as likely to be strong, positive, able, courageous and conscientious. Anxiety can affect anyone from the quiet housewife to the high-flying businessperson. It is somehow tacked on to your personality as an extra unwelcome addition. So if anxiety isn't just a state of mind, what is it?

Is anxiety a list of symptoms? If you suffer from excessive anxiety you will know how powerful and how varied the symptoms produced by your body can be. You could take the view, as many American psychologists have done, that excessive anxiety is a purely physical illness. You could certainly make out a case for this point of view, but surely there is more to excessive anxiety than a physical condition?

The nature of anxiety

You know what it's like to be anxious. It is the mental awareness of anxiety which is disturbing, but an anxiety state is more than that, it is also a state of severe physical discomfort, of sweaty palms, the possibility of diarrhoea, a shaking hand and many other purely physical symptoms which could be listed in a medical text book. To really understand anxiety you have to understand the close relationship between mind and body, because an anxiety state is a *psychological* and a *physical* condition.

Demonstrating this is quite easy. I do so in a very dramatic way when I give a talk on anxiety. Often it's a talk to a women's group, all of whom know each other and feel comfortable in each other's company. At the beginning of the talk I ask for a volunteer who somehow always turns out to be the chairperson. I ask her to sit comfortably and to relax as the audience watches. Then I attach an electrode to two of the fingers on one of her hands and these are then connected to a biofeedback monitor. This little device emits a clicking noise which becomes quieter the more she relaxes.

Once I have lulled her into a false state of security I say to her very quietly, 'Now I'm going to ask you to do some mental arithmetic.' Instantaneously the noise from the monitor rises to a scream. Fortunately for the victim I never do get round to the mental arithmetic and I am usually forgiven, but just what has triggered the reaction in the monitor? The biofeedback monitor measures the electrical conductivity of the skin. This in turn is a reflection of the moisture on the skin—if it is wet it conducts electricity more easily. It is really a measure of how much you are sweating. The thing which amazes everyone is just how rapidly the meter reacts. It seems to be instantaneous.

It is really a demonstration of the adrenalin reaction. In this case the danger the chairperson identifies isn't a charging bull or a hunting lion, it is the thought of having to do mental arithmetic in public and possibly making a fool of herself. She isn't going to be killed, yet at the instant that threat is made, adrenalin is released into the bloodstream and the body reacts instantaneously. The reaction which is measured by this machine is that of sweating, but sweating is just an example of the many other instantaneous reactions going on at the same time which would allow the individual to run away or to fight if it were necessary. Under the circumstances she might feel like doing both.

Understanding anxiety—the key

Anxiety is thus a mixture of the physical and the psychological, and that is the key, not only to understanding it, but also to *defeating* it. The association between sweaty hands and the thought of doing mental arithmetic is close and immediate. It is easy to see just how the everyday stresses of life can produce the same effect hundreds of times a day, so that in the end the unpleasant symptoms of anxiety are present all the time. Surely it is surprising, when you consider modern life, that more people aren't disabled by anxiety?

Note that the sweaty hand reaction is automatic. No one turns it on, and anyway there wouldn't be time. No one can turn it off, and you can't turn off any of these automatic responses. They are meant to be automatic, immediate and irreversible.

What do our automatic reactions do?

We have mentioned these automatic reactions previously. You will know something about them from your own experience, and you will know that they are many and varied. You will be aware of some of them, but the vast majority of these automatic reactions go on all of our lives without our knowing anything about them. They adjust our pulse-rate, our blood-pressure, the contractions of our intestine, the dilatation of our pupils, and the tension in our muscles. They also make our glands, such as our sweat or our salivary glands, function.

One of the earliest demonstrations of these reflex reactions was conducted by a man called Pavlov. He had noticed that his body produced saliva if he was hungry and he either saw or smelt food. That is to say a mental appreciation of the availability of food was translated by his body of its own accord into the production of saliva. How could this be?

Pavlov decided to do some experiments, and he used dogs as his experimental animals. He began by feeding them at the same time each day. As the dogs were fed, he rang a bell. The dogs would produce saliva when they were fed, and they came to associate the feeding with the ringing of the bell. If the bell was rung and the feeding slightly delayed, the dogs would still salivate—in response to the ringing of the bell, not to the food.

After some time the dogs would salivate when the bell was rung whether food was forthcoming or not. Their bodies had learned to associate the ringing of the bell with the provision of food, or rather their bodies had learned this reaction. It was a learned involuntary response over which the dogs had no control. The ringing of the bell was a mental concept, something experienced through the ears, not through their mouths nor their noses, yet when processed by the brain it made their bodies react and they would salivate. That kind of reaction is called a conditioned reflex, and conditioning is a form of learning. Many human reactions are like that, and they can be very complicated indeed.

Think about the simple act of crossing the road. Simple? It could hardly be more complicated. How could you compute the speed and direction of all the approaching cars, the width of the road, visibility, or the strength of the wind, and at the same time tell your legs to walk and your eyes to focus, unless most of these judgements and reactions were automatic? You look, get a sort of snapshot, and your brain does the rest like the massive computer it is. And what if the situation is complicated by the appearance of a runaway bus heading straight for you? Now you have the adrenalin reaction as well, and you have to run for your life. No time to work out all the adjustments to the function of your body which are necessary to do that. How does it all work?

The automatic nervous system

Our nervous system is divided into two parts, our voluntary nervous system and our automatic nervous system, or as it is more properly called, our autonomic nervous system. We are aware of the actions of our voluntary nervous system and we can make it do what we want it to do. If we want to lift our arm we can do that easily. But we have no voluntary control over our autonomic nervous system, which itself controls all of those bodily functions that go on all the time without us being aware of their action.

One of the problems for people suffering from anxiety is that they can become aware of some of these usually silent functions. Things get a little out of control, they go into overdrive, and instead of being automatic and silent this part of our nervous system starts to produce sensations which we do not welcome, and these sensations are worse in situations which we have learned are stressful.

The adrenal gland is part of this automatic nervous system. You might find that a little odd, but glands do react to nervous stimulation and there is nothing strange about the way your adrenal gland reacts. Adrenalin (and the similar nor-adrenalin) are the chemical transmitters of the autonomic nervous system, and the adrenal gland, located just above the kidney, produces the substance adrenalin and releases it into the bloodstream in response to the stimulation of a nerve from the brain.

See, hear, or even think danger, and the gland releases adrenalin. By using the bloodstream to distribute adrenalin the body is able to stimulate all sorts of different organs at the same time, producing a mass reaction. If this wasn't done using a substance in the bloodstream each of these organs would need a separate nerve, sometimes different kinds of nerves because each of the organs involved responds in a different way to stimulation by adrenalin.

How does it go wrong?

Learning is essential to our development, to our safety, to our ability to cross roads and deal with stress in all its forms, but what do we mean by learning? There are all sorts of learning. We can sit down and learn a poem or learn a part in a play. We can learn common sense, learn the 'rules of life in the school of hard knocks', learn to be kind and considerate, and our bodies must learn to develop appropriate physical responses as we go along. This is the way our subconscious brain develops. It is called subliminal learning and is efficient and constant.

Almost all of these reactions are beneficial, often essential. If we learn the wrong lessons, we develop the wrong reactions and our lives slowly become affected. We develop symptoms and these can be painful, embarrassing, uncomfortable or frightening. How does it happen?

Let's take an example. Many years ago a friend of mine was driving north on the M1 motorway in a hurry to get out of London. At this part of the motorway there were only two lanes and the traffic was very heavy. After a few miles he pulled out to overtake a truck, and as he did so a faster car came up behind him. To his horror he realized that the truck he was overtaking was merely the last in a line of about twenty fast-moving trucks driving nose to tail.

My friend found himself driving at the limit of his car's ability in a narrow lane between the huge, terrifying, relentless wheels of the trucks on his inside, and the crash barrier on his outside. Behind him was a long queue of angry motorists pushing him forwards. My friend, who had nearly been involved in an accident earlier that day, became panic-stricken, and for good reason. It was a frightening and potentially dangerous situation, and I should know because I was with him at the time. All that he could do was to keep his foot to the floor and watch his car inch past truck after truck.

When he eventually overtook the last truck he pulled over to the inside lane and then left the motorway altogether. He stopped the car and sat in the slip-road shaking and trying to catch his breath. After a matter of minutes he rejoined the motorway and drove north at a more leisurely speed.

That might have been the end of the affair, but he never felt completely confident driving on a motorway again, and years later at a time when his life was not running as smoothly as it might have been, and when he had begun to feel uneasy and anxious much of the time, he found that motorway driving had become a nightmare. He had suddenly developed a full-blown motorway phobia so that when he drove on the motorway he felt panicky, sick and shaky. Even the thought of motorway driving had this effect on him.

Another case study is that of a young well-brought up boy, not more than five years of age. Every Sunday he went to church with his parents and sat through the service and the sermon, but one Sunday he had a little too much orange juice before the service. He survived the first half of the service all right, but during the sermon he felt the need of a visit to the toilet, and he was too shy a child to ask to be taken out of the church. Eventually he wet his trousers. After the service, and on the way home, a friend of his parents made a joke about it and he thought that everyone would notice, and everyone would know. He was ashamed.

That feeling lingered, and he was never completely comfortable in church after that, or in any formal situation. Because his parents cared about him they stopped taking him to church. Later in his life, at a time of stress, he found that he had become extremely uncomfortable in formal situations and that he had developed the habit of avoiding them. If it became necessary to be involved in a wedding or a prize-giving or something like that, he would feel very uneasy and would develop symptoms he couldn't deal with, and which frightened him. He too had developed a phobia, excessive anxiety in a particular situation. That phobia extended to concerts and the theatre, which are similar to formal situations.

These are true stories. The people involved attributed their problems to the events I have described, and they may be right. Frightening or serious events in our lives can have after-effects, and so can a succession of small, less threatening events, each of which raises our adrenalin level just a little until it produces unpleasant symptoms which become intrusive and spoil our lives.

Being made to feel embarrassed because of our lack of social ability or shyness can over the years make our adrenalin rise in social situations to a level which causes us discomfort. That problem might be an inability to make conversation, and even a feeling that we are unattractive. It can make some situations difficult, and anxiety may develop out of them. It may take years. We may feel that our anxiety has a sudden beginning, but it has probably developed over the years until we suddenly become aware of it, as if it creeps up on us and suddenly jumps out.

Being aware of the possible cause of our problem doesn't mean that we can cure it ourselves. It isn't that simple. Our body has learned these reactions and we are stuck with them until we *unlearn* them, and we have to take active steps to do that. It's as if you were a guitar which is being tuned up to a higher and higher pitch. Initially we don't notice that anything is wrong, but at some point we become aware that we are out of tune with everyone else, and that is a very frightening, lonely feeling.

Hyperventilation

Hyperventilation just means overbreathing. So far we have talked only about the adrenalin reaction as if that was the only cause of our unpleasant symptoms, but there is at least one other possible cause. People who are nervous, who are caught in a stressful situation, can sometimes overbreathe, and that has some interesting effects on our body. When we overbreathe by panting or just breathing more deeply than usual, we blow off carbon dioxide from our lungs and this has an immediate effect on our blood chemistry. This is a very rapid reaction which fortunately is rapidly reversible, but the effect on our blood chemistry is such that it produces physical changes in our entire body similar to the ones we experience in severe anxiety.

Some doctors think that this reaction, as well as or instead of the adrenalin reaction, is the main one producing our symptoms, and for some people it might well be. It is certainly one of the things which can happen to us, but for most of us the 'hyperventilation syndrome', if it affects us at all, is only a small part of our problem and we will leave discussion of it until later.

It does however, demonstrate again the close relationship between our mind and our body. Anaesthetists prefer 'inhalational anaesthesia', which is the use of anaesthetic gasses to put us to sleep, because it is so rapid and so reversible. Switch off the gas and the patient wakes up. If you feel trapped and anxious, perhaps on an aircraft or in a lift, you may breathe a little too deeply. Your blood chemistry will change and you will develop tetany, which is a condition characterized by muscle stiffness and sometimes spasm of the hands. It is a powerful physical phenomenon, but this overbreathing is caused by a mental feeling of stress or danger.

The vicious circle

You can see how this reaction might affect us over a few years. We would begin to feel panicky and overbreathe in certain situations and thus start to feel physically tense and shaky. This sensation is very frightening, so we start to dread the situations which make us feel so ill. Eventually we avoid these situations, which makes us dread them even more.

The adrenalin reaction is just the same. In a stressful situation we produce adrenalin which makes us feel very ill. We learn to dread these frightening and disturbing symptoms which we associate with that particular situation, and we avoid that situation. It becomes increasingly difficult to face the situation because of the symptoms it produces. We are caught in the vicious circle.

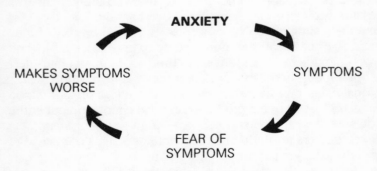

The vicious circle

Breaking the circle

We have to find a weakness in the circle. We have to break in to it, to destroy it slowly until it has lost its power. It isn't so difficult to do if you go about it the right way, but it does take determination and a little courage. You can do it.

REMEMBER:

- Excessive anxiety in some situations may be triggered by some event, or a series of small events.
- Anxiety has a mental and a physical side.
- Anxiety sets up a vicious circle.
- The circle of anxiety/symptoms/fear/avoidance/anxiety can be broken.

Chapter 4

Getting to grips with your anxiety

Anxiety is unpleasant. No one likes feeling sick and ill. No one likes the sensation of fear it produces. No one likes the feeling of loneliness and isolation which a sufferer from excessive anxiety endures. Everyone who suffers from excessive anxiety asks themselves the same questions: 'Why me? Why can't I cure myself? Why should I be scared of going to that party, or to the shops, or into a crowd when I *know* that nothing can happen to me? Why am I so stupid?'

Many of these questions have already been answered. Of course you aren't stupid because there is a logic to all of this, but it is difficult to see that logic in the everyday situations where we experience our anxiety. When we are feeling ill in a supermarket queue, there is little point in reflecting upon the place of anxiety in human evolution. It's time we got on to the practical nuts and bolts of our excessive anxiety.

We are who we are. There's no point asking ourselves 'Why me?' We start from where we are now, and right now you are a person who because of your temperament and your experience of life suffers from excessive anxiety. And you would do almost anything to banish that anxiety. You can do that, and you will. The first hurdle you have to get over is that feeling that you are stupid to fear entering these perfectly normal situations which should cause you no bother at all.

Why be afraid?

Let us get one fact absolutely straight in our minds. It would be daft to fear the supermarket queue, but that isn't what happens.

We don't fear the supermarket queue. We fear the very severe and possibly disabling physical symptoms which we experience in that queue, or at that party or whatever situation it is which causes our symptoms. That fear of your powerful symptoms is entirely logical and sensible. If someone who had no experience of an anxiety state suddenly experienced your symptoms, they would think that they were dying. It is courage which has kept you going. There is nothing illogical about your fear. The symptoms are real, and the fear and concern we have about them is just as rational and as real.

Turn back to our wheel of anxiety (page 32). The key factor in that vicious circle is that fear of your symptoms, because it is that fear which makes your symptoms worse. It is adrenalin which causes your symptoms, and some of that adrenalin is produced by your fear. But you can't stop your fear, so the wheel goes round and round. It is a logical fear, not of the situation, but of those symptoms, and no one can turn it off.

There is a way out and we have made a start. The start is always to understand what is going on, so that we can see a way into our problem. If we know that our symptoms are a natural phenomenon and that they can do us no harm, that we won't faint or cry out or whatever, then our fear must diminish just a little, and so must that adrenalin. We feel more relaxed. We have made a start.

We will still dread some situations because we will still feel bad in them. These symptoms are powerful, and the simple application of logic won't banish them. There has to be a way of controlling the symptoms themselves, so that we have less need to fear them.

Physical symptoms

All of this presupposes that you can accept that your excessive anxiety produces a collection of adrenalin-induced symptoms, but I think we have made out a good case for this already. We can't treat a condition in which we just feel unwell, and we have to do better than just saying that we feel anxious. From now on we have to be precise about our anxiety state. We really do have to pin it down. We have to know the mechanisms which make us feel so unwell. We know that our symptoms are due to adrenalin, or maybe some overbreathing, but let's consider exactly what that does to us.

Be precise

There is only one really successful way of nailing down our anxiety state. We have to take pen and paper and do some writing. We have to make lists. You will never cure an amorphous, poorly understood condition. You have to take the surgeon's scalpel to your anxiety, minutely dissect it, and examine the pieces.

Look at the situations which make your anxiety worse, and there almost certainly will be some situations which will be worse than others. It may be that you haven't realized that this is so. The situations may be subtle, and it may not be places, it may be people, or one person, or one type of person. Or it may be a type of situation, typically a situation where you feel closed in, or conspicuous.

Some people with anxiety states

It might be worth while having a look at the way excessive anxiety affects some other people. No two people are the same, so the experience of others is always of interest.

Mary

Mary was a pleasant outgoing young woman who was 28 years of age with two daughters. She had always led a full and active life. Her husband was an insurance agent and they enjoyed a good social life. They were members of a social club, and spent every Thursday night at a social evening at this club. Mary would not have considered herself to be a nervous person. She thought of herself as successful and outgoing, with no problems, although her mother had died six weeks previously.

Her day would include getting the family out to work and school, doing the housework before going to the shops. She had a regular round of calls with neighbours for coffee and had many friends and acquaintances. She would have said that she lived a full and happy life.

She began to have problems. They were minor problems at first, and she didn't think very much about them. She found that she was a little uncomfortable when she was in having coffee with a neighbour, particularly if there were a few other neighbours present. Nothing specific, nothing dramatic, just a feeling of being ill at ease. Then one afternoon whilst attending one of these coffee sessions she suddenly felt hot, as if a wave of heat had passed over her body. Her heart raced and she felt as if she was going to die.

No one seemed to notice, and she just sat quietly until the sensation had passed over her. She didn't want to make a scene. As soon as she could she made her excuses and took her leave and returned home a very worried person. She didn't mention this strange episode to anyone, not even her husband, because it seemed so odd.

Mary found that from this time on she was tense and uncomfortable at coffee sessions with her neighbours. She noticed that she had developed a tremor, so that the coffee cup rattled against the saucer. Her chest felt tight and she felt that breathing was difficult. Soon she was making excuses for not going to her neighbours' for coffee.

Her problems didn't stop there. She had another of these panic attacks at the social club. It happened in the lounge when it was full of people. She and her husband were sitting in the corner opposite the door, and when the attack came on she had to leave suddenly, crossing the full width of the room. It seemed like an interminable journey, and when her husband joined her outside to see what was wrong, all she could say was that she wanted to go home.

When they got home she tried to explain her problem to her husband, but she had difficulty finding the right words. It didn't seem to make sense. Her husband was sympathetic, and suggested that she should see her doctor, but he clearly didn't understand. Perhaps this wasn't surprising. Mary didn't really understand what was happening to her, and couldn't explain it very well to her husband. It was very perplexing. She didn't really think that she could explain it to her doctor, and was worried about what he might say, so she didn't make an appointment to see him.

The next Thursday she woke up feeling uncomfortable. She lay in bed wondering what was wrong. Then she remembered that she was going to the social club that evening. Her neck was tight and sore and her stomach was churning. She felt the way she would feel if she was worried and anxious, but what had she to be anxious about? She didn't have a worry in the world. But it was Thursday. It was social club day, and that was all it took.

That tightness lasted all day. She felt very uncomfortable and unhappy, and as the day wore on she began to feel sick. She wasn't actually sick, but she felt as if she might be sick at any time. When her husband came home form work she tried to be as normal as possible, but he realized right away that there was something wrong. By this time Mary had diarrhoea and had to make frequent trips to the toilet.

They decided not to go to the social club, and spent a quiet evening at home instead. As soon as the decision not to go to the social club had been made, Mary began to feel better. Her sickness and diarrhoea settled down and soon she felt almost normal, but as the evening wore on the tightness in her chest returned and she began to feel that she couldn't get a full breath. At one stage she went and stood at the back door trying to get some air. Later this sensation also disappeared and she went to bed feeling comfortable.

The next Thursday she woke up feeling the same way. She didn't go to the social club that night either, and it was many weeks before she was able to go back.

John

John was 45 and the sales manager of a small but very successful company. He had a staff of six salespeople working for him. He enjoyed his work and he was good at it. He knew that he would soon be promoted through the company, and he had had offers to move to a larger company with a higher salary. He had an attractive wife, three children and had no marital or financial problems. He was a happy, well-adjusted man, although recently his work had become very demanding and he was now taking work home most evenings.

John became aware that he was feeling very tense. His shoulders were sore when he was driving, and his neck was stiff and sore when he looked over his shoulder. He developed indigestion, and he felt anxious and uncomfortable. All these feelings came on over a period of a few weeks.

Slowly these feelings became more intrusive and he found that he was beginning to avoid meetings if he reasonably could. One aspect of his life became particularly bothersome. As a salesman he had to have a certain number of business lunches, sometimes with one customer and sometimes with a group of people, perhaps his own staff and representatives of a customer's company. In the morning he would scan his diary and if a lunch was

scheduled he would immediately feel sweaty and uncomfortable. As the time for the lunch approached he would feel
increasingly unwell. His stomach would churn and he would
develop a tremor. If he could make an excuse for not driving he
would ask someone else to drive for him.

When John reached the restaurant he felt very shaky indeed,
and had trouble making conversation during the drinks which
preceded the meal. The meal itself was a nightmare. He
frequently felt that he was choking and that he would have to
leave the table, but he always managed to stay. Even so he felt
conspicuous and uncomfortable and found it hard to
concentrate.

He began to be concerned about his performance in his job.
No one mentioned that he wasn't working up to standard, but
he was aware that he was finding it increasingly difficult to do
his job, and this increased his feeling of unease. He was happier
relaxing at home, but one evening he developed an annoying
feeling that he couldn't swallow. He kept trying to swallow, but
the more he tried the more he had to try, and he became rather
distressed. He felt that there was a lump in his throat which he
couldn't get rid of no matter how hard he swallowed. After a
while the feeling passed off and he became comfortable again,
but it was an unpleasant and frightening feeling while it lasted.
Eventually, after many weeks, he went to see his doctor, and after
that things started to get better.

What can we learn?

The problems these two individuals experienced were extremely
difficult. If you have excessive anxiety don't feel that you may
end up as distressed as they were because I have exaggerated
their problems in order to make a point. In describing their
difficulties I have been careful to list the actual symptoms they
experienced. I haven't just said that they felt unwell, or that they
were anxious. They had physical problems and it is the same for
you, so if you are to banish your anxiety you must find out what
these physical problems are.

Make a list

For the moment, let's do a simple exercise. Go through Mary
and John's cases with a pen and paper and make a list of their

symptoms. Whilst you are doing that, try to make out a list of the situations in which these symptoms were worst. They will have had some symptoms all of the time, but their symptoms will have been particularly troublesome in certain situations. We can discuss these lists later.

You will no doubt realize that there is a point to this exercise. What you are going to do soon is to make out a list of your own symptoms, and the situations which make them worse. That is much more difficult than making out a list for two people for whom I have given an abbreviated case history. It is much harder in real life, and you have to work at it and you have to be honest. There is a way of going about it, and we will discuss that next.

Making a diary

If your list is to be useful, you have to record just the right amount, and you have to record it at the time. Some people come to see me with a diary which contains a few words obviously written in the waiting room before the consultation. That isn't very useful. Other people come in with a book full of closely written pages containing the minutest details of their daily life. It is impossible to untangle this dissertation. You have to record just the right amount by looking at the events of your day and coming to some conclusions, and there is an art to doing that.

Make a diary like the one below. Make columns for the morning, afternoon and evening. List your symptom, *and* its severity (very mild, mild, moderate, severe or very severe. Use abbreviations.) Make a note also of any situation, event or person who might be making your symptoms worse. Here is an example:

	MORNING	AFTERNOON	EVENING
MONDAY	Stomach churning Neck tense driving to work (moderate) Business lunch today	Tense & sweaty before *lunch* (severe) Tremor at table (severe) Managed to stay	Neck sore (moderate) Reasonably comfortable (at home)

	MORNING	AFTERNOON	EVENING
TUESDAY	NO PROBLEMS	*Sales Conference* Tremor, shaky (moderate) *Showdown with Jim* tearful, couldn't swallow (severe)	Neck tense (moderate) Choking feeling: one hour

Symptom diary

You may have noticed that this diary might have been kept by John. If he kept this diary for a few weeks he would have created a basis for planning a programme of treatment for himself. Quite simply, he would know exactly what he had to treat. He wouldn't be able to treat a feeling of anxiety, or just feeling unwell, but he could begin to treat a list of symptoms.

REMEMBER:

- Anxiety can be thought of as a list of symptoms.
- It is quite logical to fear your symptoms. Physical symptoms can be treated.
- Identifying your symptoms takes time and effort.
- A diary of your symptoms can be helpful.

Chapter 5

Your symptoms—what produces them?

You are about to start keeping a diary so that you can make an accurate list of your own symptoms. You will have noticed that we have made no mention of any unresolved conflicts or underlying stresses which might be contributing to your anxiety. We are for the moment taking a purely practical approach because that is the one which gets results.

Symptom list

You have made a list of the symptoms experienced by Mary and John. Perhaps you will have recognized some of them because you experience them yourself, though hopefully you aren't too familiar with all of them. Here is a list of the ones I picked out:

Mary

Panic attacks (flushing, fast pulse)
Tense muscles
Tremor
Tightness in the chest
} Neighbours for coffee

Neck tight and sore
Churning stomach, nausea
} Prospect of going to social club

Diarrhoea
Choking, unable to swallow
} No obvious reason

John

Tense shoulder muscles
Indigestion feelings
} Driving

Feeling sweaty
Churning stomach
Tremor, feeling shaky
} Prospect of lunch
or dining

A sensation of being unable
to swallow
} No obvious reason

As I have said previously, not many people have so many symptoms at one time so this list is a bit of an exaggeration, but in real life either of these individuals could have made a similar list for themselves with the assistance of a diary. Once they had done so they would be in a position to take on their symptoms, to work at them, and to banish them.

The symptoms experienced in an anxiety state

No list of the symptoms experienced by people suffering from excessive anxiety can be complete. The following is the result of a survey I conducted a few years ago. It lists the symptoms fifty people with excessive anxiety experienced and the percentage who had each symptom. It is a fairly comprehensive list.

Panic attacks	56.4%
Muscle tension	67.3%
Pain	23.6%
Headache	49.1%
Breathing difficulty	18.2%
Swallowing difficulty	14.5%
Tearfulness	43.6%
Diarrhoea	9.1%
Excessive fatigue	47.3%
Tremor	29.1%
Dizziness	38.2%
Palpitations	40.0%
Stomach discomfort	23.6%

No one suffers from all of these symptoms at once, but sometimes one symptom can replace another. The phenomenon is called symptom transfer. When one symptom disappears another can sometimes take its place, and that can be disheartening. By the same token, when you defeat one symptom any others you may experience become easier to defeat because many of them are caused by the same physical factors. It is this physical side of your symptoms which we are going to look at next.

How are your symptoms produced?

Let's look at that list of symptoms and consider them one at a time. The reason for considering them in detail is that it is much easier to deal with something which you can understand and explain. Something which is mysterious and frightening cannot be overcome, but something which is just another symptom can be dealt with much more easily. And once a symptom is explained and you become familiar with the mechanisms which produce it, you will recognize it much earlier, and you will thus be able to deal with it much sooner. That makes the job of defeating it easier. These are some of the symptoms you might experience.

Panic attacks

We should deal with this phenomenon first because it is without any doubt the most distressing of all of the symptoms you might experience. If you have had a panic attack you will know exactly what I am talking about without any further explanation, but of course not everyone has had a panic attack.

In a panic attack everything happens. You may be standing in a queue, or maybe in an aircraft or some public place, or you might be sitting quietly at home. It might be triggered by anything, even by your thoughts. It is always disturbing, and can be very frightening. It starts suddenly. Your heart will start to hammer, your hand may shake, your stomach will churn and you will feel sweaty and faint. It is a powerful, almost overwhelming sensation.

It is caused by the sudden release of a large amount of adrenalin into the bloodstream. As you know, adrenalin has many actions on many of the body's systems, and they all come into operation at once. The effect is very disturbing.

A panic attack doesn't come out of the blue, even if that seems to be the case, but when you are familiar with the effects of a panic attack you will become aware of the events which precede it. You may begin to feel apprehensive. You may begin to sweat, to get that prickly feeling down your back, and you may notice that you are breathing more quickly than usual. You seem to be slowly losing control, and then there is this sudden explosion of sensations. You feel as if you are going to die, and all you want to do is to get out of whatever situation you are in.

Once you have had a panic attack you will not wish to repeat the experience. You will feel apprehensive in the sort of situation which might cause a panic attack, and you may well try to avoid getting into such situations. It is a very unpleasant occurrence.

We can spend more time later discussing how you can deal with panic attacks, but some things can be said straight away. Firstly, although a panic attack is very unpleasant, *it can do you no harm*. No one ever died from a panic attack. No one has ever collapsed, or fainted, or fallen down. Panic is, after all, a purely natural phenomenon. You are simply experiencing it in an unusual situation. Furthermore, a panic attack is over very quickly. If you stand quietly and breathe evenly and slowly, it will pass over in seconds.

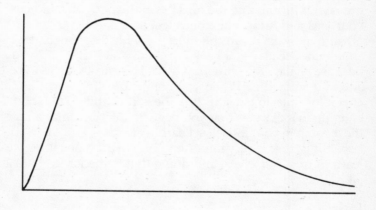

A panic attack

Why does it happen? It is just an extreme form of stress reaction. Instead of the slow steady release of adrenalin causing chronic symptoms over a period of time, there is a sudden large release of adrenalin causing sudden acute symptoms. It's the 'flight or fight' reaction again and it happens because you are in a situation which your body finds very stressful. Your automatic nervous system is triggered off, and your adrenal gland pumps adrenalin out into your bloodstream.

Despite the severity of the reaction, it is possible to control it and to manage it. With practice you should be able to have a panic attack whilst talking to someone without them being aware that you are having one. When you can do that you will rapidly lose all fear of panic attacks, and then 'hey presto!' you will stop having them. More about that later.

Muscle tension

This is the most common symptom experienced in an anxiety state. It is the basis of many other problems but may not be immediately recognized by a sufferer as such. Adrenalin secretion and overbreathing both produce muscle tension. The slow unremitting trickle of extra adrenalin over the months or years produces a slow increase in muscle tension, whilst overbreathing will do it in the short term.

Do you have increased muscle tension? Why not check? Are your shoulders raised? Is your neck stiff and sore? Is it sore if you press your thumb into the muscles at the back of your neck? Do your legs and arms sometimes feel sore and tight?

You may wake up in the morning with a sore neck and sore shoulders because you have been tense all night, and you may be tense all day. You will certainly feel physically tense in certain stressful situations. When you are next feeling uncomfortable, check for muscle tension. It is the sort of thing you should be entering in a diary so that you begin to develop an awareness of the tension in your muscles. Learning to recognize when you are becoming tense is very important, because it is one thing we can learn to treat ourselves, and doing that is the key to banishing all our anxiety.

Pain

Anxious people often feel pain. It can be severe enough to be annoying and disturbing. It is usually caused by muscle spasm. You know how painful a stitch can be, or a cramp in the leg? They are caused by muscle spasm, and if your muscles are tense and sore anyway, you are much more likely to suffer a strain, or to just experience pain from tight muscles. You might experience pain in the small muscles between your ribs, or in your neck or back, or you may have aching limbs. It is all muscular.

There are other kinds of pain and other sources of pain. Too much acid in your stomach will produce indigestion-type pain and this can be related to stress and anxiety. Some types of bladder or bowel pain can be caused by spasm in the special muscles involved in these bodily functions. If you are having that sort of pain your doctor may be able to help, and we will talk about that later.

Headache

Is there a tense person who hasn't had a headache? Headaches can be devastatingly severe, and can last for days. What causes the tension headache? The next time you have a headache try pressing your thumb into the muscles in the back of your neck. You will find hot spots of pain which will lift the top of your head off if you press them. You will be able to detect little nodules in your neck muscles. It is our old friend muscle spasm again. Most head pain comes from tension in neck muscles, some of which will contract into those nodules which are so tender. Like all forms of muscle tension, it is treatable.

There are other kinds of headache, some of which are treatable by your doctor. You might have migraine, or sinusitis, and even the most relaxed person in the world can have them, but they have particular characteristics of their own. If your neck muscles are tense and sore to touch, you are having a tension headache and it is related to your increased anxiety.

Breathing difficulty

Some people with increased anxiety find that there are occasions when they feel that they just can't get a breath. They take a deep breath and try to fill their lungs, but they don't seem able to breathe deeply enough to get a satisfactory intake of air. It becomes quite disturbing and they may open a window or go to the door in order to get a breath.

This sensation is quite unlike asthma, where the actual breathing tubes close down and it is difficult to breathe in or out. In this case it is just a sensation that you cannot get a full breath even though the air does enter your lungs freely. It is caused by tightness in the small muscles between your ribs, the intercostal muscles. Tightness in these muscles gives you a very odd, but very characteristic sensation. It is disturbing, but it can do you no harm.

Swallowing difficulty

Like the problem with breathing, this is more of an unpleasant sensation than an actual difficulty. You feel that one swallow isn't enough. It's as if there is a ball stuck in your throat. You have to keep swallowing in an effort to get rid of it. It can be frightening and unpleasant.

It's a problem that has been known about for years, and like many ancient problems it has an ancient Latin name (via the Greek word for *womb*, *hystericos*). It is called a *Globus Hystericus*. The word hystericus doesn't imply that the sufferer is hysterical, just that the condition has a psychological cause. You have a psychological ball in your throat; it is very interesting to know that the Ancients had some insight into what we tend to think of as a modern condition.

And the mechanism which causes our Globus Hystericus? You should be able to work it out by now. It's worse when you are in company, when you are being observed or when you are nervous and tense. It is caused by tension in the muscles involved in the swallowing process. They get tight and you feel that you can't swallow.

Tearfulness

There are all sorts of tears. There are tears of joy and tears of sorrow. You can feel tearful and sad when you are depressed, but that isn't what we are thinking about with the sort of tearfulness you experience when you are anxious. It is important to make the distinction between being depressed and tearful and being anxious, tense and tearful.

If you are depressed you should see your doctor and get medical help. If you are depressed you will feel sad, unable to lift your mood, unable to see the future, unhappy. You may have other things like finding that you wake up early in the morning, and you may feel worse at some times of the day than at others, but if you are anxious you will feel anxious and tense, and your tears may be tears of frustration rather than of sadness.

You may feel tearful in company, in stressful situations and in situations where you feel conspicuous. You feel as if you are losing control, as if you are going to break down and cry in public. It is almost as if the tears are being squeezed out by the tightness of the muscles around your eyes. It is a very distressing symptom just because of this feeling that you are losing control and that something may happen which other people will notice.

Diarrhoea

Anyone who has had to make a speech knows that feeling of butterflies in the stomach which precedes that dreaded moment when we take to our feet and begin to speak. Anyone who has had an interview knows the same feeling. Some people get it more often, perhaps before going out to a party or to a meeting, or at other times when it doesn't seem to be appropriate. It can be more than a sensation. You can actually have diarrhoea, and it can happen to some people every time they start to leave the house, and in that situation it is quite a serious symptom. How does it occur?

Diarrhoea has another medical name. It is called intestinal hurry, and that name describes it very well. There is a wave of contraction along the entire length of our intestine which carries the contents of our intestine along. It is co-ordinated and it moves at a set rate so that the contents of our gut can be processed as they travel along, like an internal conveyor belt. The last function of this conveyor is the absorption of water which happens in the last part of the bowel, the rectum, and it is here that our stools turn from liquid to solid.

If this wave of contractions is speeded up, the contents of the gut are swept along and the normal functions, including the absorption of water, haven't time to occur. We get that familiar feeling of diarrhoea, and we may even pass a loose stool, or sometimes pure water. All sorts of things produce diarrhoea. An infection of the bowel will do it, and this is usually a virus of the sort that gives you holiday diarrhoea. An injection of adrenalin has been shown to do it experimentally, and the secretion of adrenalin from your own adrenal gland will do it in times of stress.

For some people, just leaving the house is stressful enough to do it, for others it may be going out to a social event. The sort of diarrhoea produced in these circumstances is slightly different from the diarrhoea of gastro-enteritis. It is less severe and easier to control. It tends to be more of a loose stool than the high pressure diarrhoea of a bowel infection. It is unpleasant, but it isn't disabling and the fear of its social effects may be worse than the diarrhoea itself. This is again a real, but controllable symptom.

Excessive fatigue

Many people come to see me and all GP's with the same complaint. They say that they are tired all the time. They have no energy. They sleep well, but they wake up tired, and they remain tired all day. Some feel that they can't take any more. When asked, they have no idea why they might be so tired. They aren't working any harder. They are getting to bed at the right time, but it doesn't make any difference. They are simply tired all the time.

If you feel fatigued all the time there is probably one simple reason. You feel tired because you *are* tired. But why should you be tired if you are getting a good night's sleep? If you were getting a good night's sleep you probably wouldn't feel tired, but are you getting the good sleep you think you are? Ask yourself these questions. Do you wake up feeling tired? Is your neck stiff and sore in the morning? Is your jaw sore from teeth clenching during your sleep? Are there nail marks in the palms of your hands from clenching your fists during the night? If the answer to any of these questions is yes, then you haven't had a restful sleep. Your eyes may have been closed all night, but that is as far as it goes.

You may have been tense all night. Your body can tolerate tension for quite a long time, but eventually it begins to have physical effects, and the first of these is the real sensation of tiredness. You feel tired all the time.

Tremor

Many anxious people have a shaky hand. So do many people who aren't anxious at all, but if you are anxious you are more likely to have a tremor. Why does your hand shake? Clench your fist tightly. Hold it clenched and it will begin to shake due to the tension in the muscles in your arm; so your tremor is due to muscle tension. When you are relaxed it will go away.

Dizziness

You can be dizzy for all sorts of reasons. If you were to ask your doctor why you feel dizzy he or she would want to know much more about the actual sensation you are experiencing, because there are different kinds of dizziness.

If you have a sensation of things rotating, if you vomit or if you fall over, then your dizziness must be due to a problem with the balance mechanism in your middle ear. If by dizziness you mean that you feel unsteady, that you feel one-sided, or off-centre, and if you also feel tense and anxious, then there is every chance that your sensation of dizziness is due to tension in the muscles on one side of your neck.

Your neck muscles are involved in your sensation of balance. If you are tense on one side of your neck, then you will feel that you are leaning towards that side. Do the test. Push your thumb into the muscles on the affected side. If they are extremely sore, then this may well be the reason why you are feeling dizzy. It is an unpleasant sensation, but you won't fall over or make a fool of yourself. You will just feel a little off-centre, and that will do you no harm.

Palpitations

Palpitations are rapid heart beats, or more likely a series of extra heart beats each followed by a pause, a space where the early beat should have been, so that it seems as if the heart has an irregular rate. It is a very unpleasant sensation. There is a funny feeling in the left side of the chest and it is very easy to believe that there is something serious going on. That isn't the case.

These irregular beats are caused by the direct action of adrenalin on the heart. It is just another physical aspect of your anxiety, and like every other aspect of that anxiety it can do you no physical harm. There is nothing whatsoever wrong with your heart. You are producing too much adrenalin, that's all.

Of all the symptoms mentioned so far, this is the one most easily treated by medication. Palpitations can be controlled by drugs called Beta (β)-blockers. These drugs do what their name suggests, they block the Beta, or cardiac actions of adrenalin. More about that in a later chapter. If you are suffering from palpitations, see your doctor.

Stomach discomfort

Stomach discomfort can be caused by having too much acid in your stomach, and the reason for that is too much adrenalin. It can give you indigestion. That is one sort of stomach discomfort.

Another type of stomach discomfort, and it is really abdominal discomfort felt lower down, is due to something we have talked about before. Remember those contractions carrying the contents of the gut through our abdomens? The contractions have to be co-ordinated if they are to work efficiently, and if they don't work efficiently we can become very uncomfortable.

If we are anxious many of the things which our autonomic nervous systems do automatically go slightly wrong. It is our autonomic (or automatic if you prefer) nervous system which sets the level of tension in our muscles, and if this goes wrong it causes many of the problems we have discussed. It also causes an upset in the co-ordination of our gut muscles which produces several different symptoms. Often it is distension of our abdomens, causing some women to complain that they are bigger round the middle than when they were pregnant. This can be accompanied by either diarrhoea or constipation, and often by crampy pain and flatulence.

These symptoms are collectively called the irritable bowel syndrome, which can be a physical manifestation of anxiety and which will do you no harm. Banish your anxiety, and it will disappear.

Other symptoms

There are many other possible symptoms associated with anxiety. Some men may have bladder problems such as having pain after passing water and the dribbling of urine, again due to spasm in certain muscles. There can be bowel pain and all sorts of things, but there is always a logical explanation, and often it is due to muscle spasm.

Anxious people can of course have other illnesses, and it would be wrong to attribute every symptom to anxiety. Bladder symptoms might be due to an infection, for example. If you are worried about a symptom and can't explain it, do see your doctor. But if he or she is happy that there is no other illness present, think of a physical reason associated with your anxiety and the physical mechanisms which might be producing it. Later on we will discuss ways of managing your symptoms and ultimately banishing them.

Now you must start to have a look at your own symptoms, even if at the moment you might not even be aware that you have any. Perhaps you are just not feeling well. You can't deal with that. You have to be more specific. Get back to that diary and start writing. Your diary, and the use you put it to, is crucial to your efforts to banish your anxiety, so it is worth saying some more about it.

Your diary is for your own use. It's a way of screwing a handle on to your anxiety, giving you something to get hold of so that you can start to reel in your anxiety and get it under control.

If you aren't too good at keeping a diary don't worry—just do the best you can. Try to write a few words about your problem. Try to make a list of your symptoms at a given time, say in the morning, or write a few words about the way you feel just as if you were writing to a friend. Say: 'When I got up this morning I felt shaky and sick. When I got on the bus my hand was trembling...' and so on. You want to give your anxiety a form, as if you were describing an old enemy, because that's just what you are doing. Enemies are there to be defeated, and anxiety, your enemy, exists in many physical forms. *Nail it.*

Try to do a little more than just make a list of symptoms. Do one more little exercise. When you have some sort of a list of your symptoms and the situations which make them worse, try to also make a note of what mechanism has produced them. Is it that the room has been too hot, so that you have been sweating and that this discomfort has been translated by your body into anxiety? Has your stomach been churning through hunger, and has this led to discomfort and anxiety? Have you been too cold? Have you been bored? Has there been something special about the situation, perhaps concern about a lift home? If it happened in the cinema, was the music too loud and the images disturbing? If it was a party, did you really dislike the people there, and did that make you uncomfortable?

The more you can discover about your anxiety the better, and the easier it will be to banish it. You have to know and understand your enemy, so you need to be thinking straight. Once you start to notice things about your life, you will find it easier to understand the details of your anxiety. It will go from a frightening panicky affliction to a dynamic system of life events and physical sensations with logical cause and effect mechanisms. When you have got a handle on your anxiety you can begin to control it, but you have to go about that in a logical and sensible way.

REMEMBER:

- Anxiety produces physical symptoms.
- Understanding how your symptoms are produced makes them less frightening.
- There are many kinds of different symptoms.
- Almost all of your symptoms are produced by having too much adrenalin in your bloodstream.
- Muscle tension is often the physical reason why you feel bad.
- Keeping a diary helps you pin down your symptoms.

Chapter 6

Learning to treat your anxiety

It is said that knowledge is power, and you have spent a lot of time acquiring knowledge of your anxiety, about what it is and how it works. You are making a study of your own anxiety so that you will come to know it intimately. Now the time has come for you to take on your anxiety, to confront the old enemy.

Perhaps confront isn't the right word to use. Confrontation produces adrenalin as you will know very well. No, we need to sneak up on our anxiety, to plan our campaign carefully so that we progress in slow stages. We don't want to ruffle any feathers, particularly if they are our own. We need a strategy, and we need a weapon. Both are available.

More about your diary

Planning any strategy requires a pencil and paper. You are making notes about the activities of your anxiety state in the form of a diary, about what symptoms you have and what situations make them worse. Please do this. It's easy to read a book such as this, but if you are to succeed you really have to do what it says and actively take on your anxiety state. You can't just wish it away. You have to do something about it, and the first step is to keep that diary, even if doing so isn't as easy as it sounds.

The first thing you should try to do with your diary is to identify your starting point. You have to find some aspect of your anxiety which you want to banish, and which isn't too difficult. In other words it has to be an attainable goal. It has to be something which causes you problems, but problems which aren't too severe. And if it's something which you can practice over and over again so much the better.

It might be travelling to work in the train. Perhaps that is something which you have to do every morning and which gives you unpleasant symptoms. If so, study it. What is it about your journey which gives you the symptoms? Are they there when the train is empty? Do you become tense and have a fast heart rate when the train pulls into a station and a lot of people get on? And what about those symptoms? Do you get feelings of diarrhoea, do you sweat or do you get muscle tension? Do you overbreathe? Make a list of your symptoms.

You might be a housewife who experiences symptoms in shops. The supermarket queue might be a nightmare. Don't start trying to solve your problems of the supermarket queue because that might be too difficult for a beginner. You can do that later. Try the corner shop first. Try to find somewhere which isn't too threatening, where your symptoms aren't too severe, and best of all somewhere where you can go every day.

Anything will do. It might be a lift which you tend to avoid. It might be that you cross the road to avoid dogs or cats, or you might not feel comfortable in a wind. There is no limit to the things which can cause problems. Nothing is too bizarre, too strange or improbable. Choose something relatively easy and attainable, and make the decision.

Decide that you are going to tackle your problem, and if you do that I will give you the weapon to use.

What can you do?

The way that you treat the symptoms of anxiety is probably the opposite of what you might think. When people begin to feel anxious they tend to try to defeat it by doing something active. The housewife may begin to clean the house furiously, trying to distract herself from her symptoms. Someone else who is becoming anxious prior to going out will pace up and down, thus winding himself up, churning out adrenalin. That isn't the best approach. Do the opposite. Slow down. Just stop what you're doing and relax. That sounds simple, but for the tense, anxious person, it may be the most difficult thing in the world.

How do you relax?

Do you remember how I used a biofeedback monitor to demonstrate to an audience how quickly your autonomic nervous system can react? You really have very little control over it at all, and that includes having control over your muscle tension. Yet muscle tension is behind so many of the unpleasant sensations we experience when we are anxious. If we could just control our muscle tension we would have made a good start along the road to controlling the symptoms of anxiety. Relaxation is something we have to learn. Just sitting in front of the TV trying to relax isn't going to get you anywhere because you can be tense even when you are asleep, so relaxation is a skill we have to actively acquire.

It is impossible to be physically relaxed and still be mentally tense. So there is a double pay-off to relaxation. Not only does it help you to control most of the unpleasant sensations associated with anxiety, it also relaxes the mind. The problem is that it isn't easy to do.

What is relaxation?

It is perhaps easier to say what relaxation isn't. It isn't just sitting watching television. It isn't even dozing in a chair. You can be fast asleep all night and still wake up tense and sore. Relaxation is a skill which has to be learned, rehearsed and constantly practised. It is a skill to be learned and then used. It is the antithesis of tension, and your main weapon against it.

At the moment you have no weapons. Your body runs your life. You are a slave to it and it makes you miserable. Relaxation isn't the answer to all your problems, but learning to relax is a very efficient start because it puts you back in control, and you may have begun to think that you would never be in control again. You can relax physically, and you can be calm mentally. You have everything to play for.

Just like the task of keeping your diary, you have to do some work if you want to learn how to relax. You will find it disappointingly difficult and it will take time, but it is possible for anyone, no matter how tense they may be now, to learn how to relax. It is worth the effort.

Relaxation exercises

If you want to learn how to relax, start by practising at a time when you are reasonably comfortable and in a place where relaxation will be easy, since you can't start to learn when you are stressed and tense, though you will be able to use relaxation to control these sensations later. Allow at least twenty minutes and make sure that you use a warm and private room. Either sit in a comfortable chair with your head supported or else lie on a bed. I prefer to sit because it is more like the real situations you will meet outside.

You must practise conscientiously every day until you have mastered the technique. That is of the utmost importance, so don't give up or be impatient. It will take you at least two weeks and you may feel at times that you aren't getting anywhere. You are, and you will, even if it seems to take a long time.

When you achieve relaxation you will know because you will feel warm, comfortable, sleepy and . . . relaxed! It is a pleasant, almost forgotten sensation. It is worth working for because it has two uses. Firstly, it can be used as a weapon against muscle tension and that is something you will be very pleased to have in many situations. It will open the door to a new way of life. Secondly, it will make you aware of when you are getting tense much earlier than you currently do. Indeed you may not be aware that you are tense at all until you learn what relaxation is like. In the real world where you tend to feel anxious, the earlier you become aware of the tension in your muscles and thus become aware of the need to do something about it, the easier it will be to reverse.

So choose your warm room and make the time. No excuses . . . ever. Read and learn the exercises I am going to describe, or if you have difficulty, record them on a cassette and do them to the sound of your own voice, making sure that you speak slowly and that the exercises take twenty minutes.

Sit comfortably with your head supported. Breathe slowly and evenly and either close your eyes or look at an object in the distance. Slow your breathing some more and relax.

Hands and arms

Start the exercises with your arms and hands. Start with your right hand by clenching your right fist. Hold it clenched for a moment and notice the sensations that clenching it produces not only in your hand but in your lower arm. The palm of your hand, your knuckles and the back of your hand will feel tight as will your lower arm. Hold that for a second and then suddenly relax your fist, letting your fingers hang down. Your hand and arm will now feel warm and heavy and relaxed. Keep your breathing slow and then slow it even more.

Now go to your left hand and repeat the exercise exactly as for the right hand, concentrating hard on the sensations produced by first clenching and then relaxing, and notice the heaviness and warmth in your hand after you have finished. Slow your breathing.

Shoulders and neck

If you are habitually tense your shoulders are often hunched and sore. Concentrate on your shoulders now. Tighten them up and hold them in that uncomfortable raised position for a second or two, noticing the tension in your shoulders, neck and in the top part of your chest and back. Now, just as before, suddenly relax these muscles and let your arms and shoulders hang down. Notice the feeling of relaxation in your shoulders, back, chest and neck. Slow your breathing.

Now concentrate on your neck. Tense your neck muscles by pushing your head back until you can feel tension in the muscles in the front of your neck, but be careful not to push too hard. Again, relax your neck suddenly and notice the feeling of relaxation in the muscles. Move your head around so that it feels floppy and heavy and slow your breathing as before.

Face muscles

Now tighten the muscles of your face. Frown and close your eyes as tightly as you can. Then increase the tension by clenching your teeth tightly, pressing your lips together and pressing your tongue into the roof of your mouth. Your whole face will feel tense, so when you suddenly relax these muscles you will notice how your forehead, cheeks, jaw and lips feel loose. Let your jaw sag slightly and slow your breathing. You may now, with experience and practice, be starting to feel comfortable, warm, heavy and drowsy.

Back and stomach

Now move on down your body. Arch your back slightly and pull in your tummy. Hold that tension for a few moments until you are aware of the feeling of tension in the muscles of your back and stomach. Make yourself as thin as you can. Now relax these muscles slowly and note what that feeling of relaxation is like in the muscles of your back and stomach. Take time to enjoy the sensation.

Feet and legs

Start with your right leg. Straighten your leg and push your foot and toes away from you, and as before note the tension in your toes, foot and lower leg. Hold that tension and then relax it suddenly so that your foot and lower leg feel loose. Pause to enjoy the sensation before repeating the exercise with your left leg. Then slow your breathing and stay in position.

Finishing off

Now you must really concentrate on your breathing. Slow it down to about eight respirations per minute and note that your arms and legs are heavy. Your hands will feel warm and your tummy, back, neck and face will feel soft.

Think of a calm relaxing scene such as a warm beach or a warm bed, and think the word 'calm'. Breathe in and out slowly, and as you breathe out think that word 'calm'. Do that about twenty times. If you have achieved deep relaxation, you will know. It is a very different state from what you are used to, almost equivalent to self-hypnosis. Enjoy it.

When you are ready, finish the session gradually. Move your arms and legs and count down from 10 to 1. Say out loud: 10..9..8..7..6. .5..4..3..2..1..Wake Up!

Problems

The first and most obvious problem is that you may have difficulty achieving relaxation. It isn't easy. Try making a tape and relaxing to that, and make sure that you aren't disturbed and that you have the time to learn the technique, and remember that it will take time. If you can't achieve perfect relaxation don't worry, if you can ease the tension in your muscles at all that will be a help.

If you are particularly good at relaxing you may fall asleep before the end of your session. That isn't a major problem, but try not to do it. You want to be in control of your relaxation and you can't be in control if you're asleep. However, if you have trouble sleeping you can use relaxation to help you to get to sleep at night.

Your worst problem may be that you will relax adequately during your relaxation session, but as soon as you stand up and move about you become tense again. That is a common experience so don't worry about it. Remember that you are learning a skill which you can use in difficult situations, so that achieving relaxation only when you really want to is a valuable asset. You want to be able to call up your relaxation at will, maybe in a meeting or on a bus or train, and that is something you can learn to do. It doesn't matter if the sensation of relaxation doesn't persist, though with experience and practice you should become generally more relaxed.

Using relaxation

You must work at your relaxation; it is important for your recovery. Remember that with practice you will be able to notice when you are becoming tense sooner than you otherwise would, and so deal with it before it becomes troublesome. Dealing with your muscle tension requires the skill of relaxation. Of course you may not be able to go through all the tightening and relaxing procedures in a public place, but you don't have to. You can take short cuts in public, working towards the sensation of relaxation you have learned in private.

Work through the exercises in your mind, relaxing your hands and arms, shoulders, neck and face and so on. Relax them in turn until you have achieved relaxation and remember your breathing. If all else fails you can simply slow your breathing.

Remember that relaxing your body relaxes your mind.

Breathing exercises

Overbreathing can cause muscle tension by changing the chemistry of your blood. This is different from the sort of panicky breathing which you might experience in a crisis. It is a chronic condition which can contribute to your day to day anxiety by making you tense. You may breathe faster than normal, breathe more deeply than normal, or you may have developed the habit of sighing frequently. In fact all of these things are all a matter of habit. Bad habits can be replaced by better habits, and you can learn to breathe more correctly. It takes effort but it can be done by practising breathing exercises.

For these exercises you don't need a private room. They are perhaps best practised whilst watching TV. If you are watching with someone else you had better explain what you are doing. To learn these exercises sit in a semi-reclining position, slouched and leaning back in a comfortable armchair. Relax.

When you are at rest you breathe with your tummy muscles. That seems strange but it is true, as you are about to find out. It is only when you are exercising that you use your chest muscles to raise and lower your ribs, forcing the air in and out of your lungs. If you are using these chest muscles in your semi-reclining position you are overbreathing.

In order to find out what is going on place one hand on your chest, and the other one on your tummy. That's all you have to do. When you are in this position, notice which of your hands is moving. If it is your tummy hand you are breathing normally, but if it is your chest hand, you are overbreathing. Notice if you are taking frequent sighs.

Now all you have to do is to breathe slowly and quietly, trying to let your tummy hand do the work. Try not to sigh or to breathe too rapidly. Just let yourself relax and breathe normally. Stay in this position as long as possible because these skills are not learned quickly. You should spend the evening taking notice of your breathing, and as many weeks as it takes to break the habit of incorrect breathing. You are trying to develop an awareness of something which is usually automatic, but which for you may have gone slightly wrong so that it has become set at too high a level, like an inaccurate thermostat.

To change your breathing habit you first have to develop an awareness of just what is happening, and then control it if it has gone wrong. With the passage of time and with practice your breathing will become automatic again, but this time at the 'correct setting.' The same is true for the tension in your muscles when you have learned to relax. You have to reset that tension, using your relaxation exercises.

What now?

Now you have to practise, to work at the tasks which have been set. You have to gain control of these functions which have gone wrong, and you have to become proficient at the exercises so that you can use them effortlessly when you most need them. Taking them out of your home and into the big world outside is the most difficult thing of all to do.

You are now in the business of controlling the physical manifestations of your anxiety in the knowledge that if you can do that, you can stop feeling the mental awareness of your anxiety. The way forward is clear. You now have the tools to do what you have to do. You are keeping a diary, studying your daily problems in detail. Now you have to put it all together.

REMEMBER:

- You have to relax actively. That means doing exercises.
- You cannot be physically relaxed and mentally tense.
- Overbreathing can also make you tense.
- You can use relaxation techniques in difficult situations.
- You can regain control of your body.

Chapter 7

Putting it together

Progress down the difficult road to recovery can be maddeningly slow, but what else can we expect? Your anxiety didn't appear overnight, and it won't go away overnight, but it will go away and that is a certainty.

I hope that you already understand much of the disturbing things that have been happening to you, and that they have been demystified. You can now accept that some frightening or worrying things are just an exaggeration of normal physical reactions. You know something about the anxiety which afflicts you every day—what it is, what brings it on and keeps it going—because you have kept a careful diary of your symptoms and the situations which make them worse. You know how to control some of the physical symptoms of anxiety, and you know that that will relax your mind. Now you want to get on with your life, a life without anxiety.

Relaxation isn't the only weapon you will have to defeat your anxiety. In the next chapter we will talk about other methods of helping yourself. You can attack this problem from many angles, but let's take one thing at a time. Just for now let's stick to the skills we have already learned, and see how we can use them in our everyday lives.

Using your new techniques

You have now learned some of the techniques you can use against anxiety, but you may also have discovered that actually using them is much more difficult than you thought it would be. How can you put them into action?

Let's start with your diary. Has it told you anything you didn't know? It certainly should have filled in the details of your anxiety state. You knew that you were anxious, now you want to know exactly where your anxiety is bad, exactly how bad it is in that particular situation, and what or who triggers it off. You want to know the dynamics of your anxiety because your anxiety is a learned reaction, and it is nurtured and sustained by the events of your everyday life. If you want to unlearn it you have to know all about these events and the way they produce your symptoms.

Can I suggest that you go back to your pen and paper? Remember that we are going to begin our assault on our anxiety by selecting a situation which is only moderately threatening. Use your diary to choose such a situation, and then think how you can use your relaxation to defuse the triggering points. Begin by writing all that you can about the situation you want to tackle. The best way to understand how to do this is to consider an example, and that is what we will do now. We will consider a bad case, someone with very disturbing problems, but solvable problems nonetheless.

Desmond

Desmond was a young man who worked in a design office. He seemed to be a clever, ambitious person, married but with no children as yet. He was successful and good at his job, but when he came to see me he was in despair. Things had begun to go wrong, and he saw his career and all of his hopes collapsing around him. He felt anxious all the time, and his problem was so desperate that he thought he was actually going mad.

You will know how we proceeded. Once I was sure of the nature of Desmond's problem, I was able to explain to him the reasons for much of what was happening and he gained a lot of help from that alone. He realized that he wasn't going mad, and that he wasn't the only person in the world to suffer from the problems produced by increased anxiety. He was told that there were things that he could do about his condition and was taught relaxation exercises. He went away much happier than he had been when he first arrived.

He couldn't come to any conclusions about the nature of his anxiety except for realizing that he didn't feel well. He didn't think in terms of symptoms, and he didn't think in terms of difficult situations, so he agreed to keep a diary, which he did in an elegant hand on a professional drawing pad. When he came back to see me he had a lot of information for us to discuss.

Desmond had many problems, but he was able to discuss them cheerfully—quite a contrast to his first visit. From his account of his personal life, work and social life we picked out some areas which seemed amenable to treatment and on which we could make a start. Some social occasions were very difficult, and we simply ignored them at that time. We could tackle them later. The areas we started on were also areas of particular importance for Desmond because they affected his work. By this time Desmond had discussed his problems with his wife and explained them to her, and she was sympathetic, understanding and probably not a little relieved. There were two areas we decided to tackle, his journey to work and a problem he had with meetings.

Problem one: going to work

The first was the problem of going to work. That was difficult every morning, but worse on Thursdays. What actually happened in the morning? Desmond set out to find the answers. This was his typical morning: he hated the thought of going to work so he would postpone it till the last minute, getting up late and having a rushed breakfast. He would feel shaky and his tummy would always be upset. Before going out he would have to go into the toilet where he would have diarrhoea, and that would really start his problems. He would have the continuing sensation of diarrhoea and so wouldn't be confident enough to leave the house. Instead he would walk up and down the hall, holding his abdomen. He would go back into the toilet three or four times. Eventually he would leave the house and run to the bus stop. Sometimes things were so bad he had to take a later bus.

Once on the bus he would feel a little better, but would still be shaky and uncomfortable. He had to change buses at the depot, and there was a toilet there so he felt more confident as he approached it. He had never had to use this toilet, but it was nice that there was one handy. His second bus journey was a nightmare. As he approached his office he would feel shaky and would develop a tremor which he felt everyone would notice. On bad days he was even uncertain about his ability to walk.

And what about Thursdays? On Thursday there was a Unit Meeting held in the Director's office. On Thursday Desmond would wake up feeling apprehensive, wonder why, and then remember—it was Thursday, meeting day. Last Thursday

Desmond had had a panic attack. He was sure he couldn't go back to the meeting again.

The journey

The journey was something which Desmond really wanted to sort out because he had to get to work every day. He had every motivation to do something about it, and he was prepared to work at his relaxation and breathing exercises if they were going to help.

The first thing we did had nothing to do with relaxation or breathing. Desmond was given some simple and apparently obvious advice, but then most advice in these circumstances is obvious—to everyone that is except the person who is receiving it. Desmond was so bound up in his problems, so anxious and frightened by what was happening to him and by what might happen to him in the future, that nothing was obvious to him. He received reassurance from the explanation of his condition and the knowledge that he wasn't alone, and he welcomed the advice offered.

He was getting up in the morning at the last moment, really because he was postponing the awful reality of his day. He was advised to get up half an hour earlier and to avoid rushing— rushing pumps up the adrenalin. He was advised to slow down, to move more slowly and breathe more slowly, to have a breakfast, and after breakfast to sit down and do his relaxation exercises. By relaxing his voluntary muscles in his arms, legs and neck he was helping to relax the involuntary muscles of his body, and these included the muscles of his gut which worked in overdrive in the morning and gave him the sensation of impending diarrhoea.

He made one journey to the toilet. The act of having a bowel movement stimulates other muscles and can make one feel shaky and uncomfortable as we all know, and it can produce a further feeling of diarrhoea so that the more you go the more you want to go. Desmond was advised to return to the living room and to sit relaxing for a few minutes, avoiding an immediate return to the toilet. If he had to go back he could, but he was to delay his return for as long as possible. In fact, to his surprise, he was able to avoid going back at all after a few days' practice. After this morning period of relaxation, when he was as settled as possible, he would leave the house and head for the bus stop.

Desmond understood that the diarrhoea he experienced

wasn't like real diarrhoea, and that he had some control, so his bus journey became less of a nightmare and whatever anxiety he still experienced could be controlled by relaxing on the bus. His worst problem now was getting on to the bus in the first place. Waiting at the stop was bad. He had all sorts of doubts about his ability to deal with his change, and even how his legs would work. Again it was control of his breathing and his relaxing which helped him. On the second leg of his journey he needed as much relaxation as he could muster as he approached his office.

Something else was of help to him. He was able to use his relaxation sessions at home to good advantage. He had a good imagination, and at the end of his relaxation session when he was thinking 'calm' he would imagine his journey in detail, stop by stop. He found that his body would produce the same physical sensations as he would experience on the real journey, and he could use his relaxation and his 'calm' to control them. He was using his relaxation sessions to desensitize himself to the trauma of his journey.

We have introduced two new ideas, *reorganization* and *desensitization*. You can reorganize events in your day, not to avoid difficulties, which would be quite wrong, but to manage them more easily. You can practise difficult situations either in your imagination, or preferably by doing them in real life as frequently as possible, and thus by frequent exposure to them remove the fear of the unpleasant sensations you have been experiencing. This is called desensitization; more about it later.

Problem two: the meeting

In Desmond's everyday life the Thursday meeting was the most traumatic event. He could only practise it once a week and that wasn't often enough to allow his body to become used to it. It was held in a room which made Desmond uncomfortable, and worst of all, he had had a panic attack. Now his anxiety was at a peak, too high to be able to control it with simple relaxation. He had real problems.

His problems weren't insoluble, even though they were difficult. He was advised to go back to the meeting if he felt that he reasonably could, and was told that a panic attack, though frightening, could do him no harm and that if he had another he was to try to stay in the room and let the panic attack flow over him. If he couldn't do that he was to leave quietly without making excuses or drawing attention to himself.

The next step was to look in detail at the meeting itself, and of course that required the detailed notes he had kept in his diary. What happened at the meeting? Why was it so upsetting? The answer was that it wasn't just a meeting, it was a performance, because Desmond had to give a report, and at that time all his colleagues would be watching him. It was also a test, because what was said about his report was a judgment on his work for the week. The meeting was physically demanding because it was held in a small hot room, and his immediate boss was an unsympathetic, competitive individual who liked to keep his juniors up to the mark by the use of sarcasm. No wonder Desmond found it difficult. But what could he do about it?

For the moment let's stick to the weapon we know best, that of using relaxation techniques to defuse the situation. In the next chapter we can discuss other equally important techniques such as reorganizing, desensitizing, social skills training and the place of rehearsal and practice. All of these techniques are applicable to Desmond's situation. Before you can use any of them you have to understand the dynamics of the situation you find threatening.

Desmond practised relaxation exercises every day, and when he had mastered the technique, which took a week, he was able to put it to practical use without even leaving his house. Remember that he could practise his journey in real life every day—he had to if he wanted to get to work. His meeting was a weekly event so he couldn't practise that often enough to be able to develop any real skills in managing it.

Just like before, he had to use his imagination. After his relaxation session he would think 'calm', and then go through the events of the last meeting in detail, just as if he was actually there. He would begin with his arrival at the building, go through the morning until it was time for the meeting, and then recreate that meeting in his mind and actually experience the sensations he normally had at the real meeting. When things began to get out of hand he could slow them down, think 'calm' and relax. As he was in control of the situation he was able to look at it, to distance himself from it and see what things made him worse.

He found that his degree of anxiety was affected by who was present. If his boss was away and his deputy was present, Desmond wasn't nearly so anxious. The position of his seat was important. He always tried to sit near the door, but if that seat was taken he became more anxious. If his report wasn't properly prepared he would be more anxious. If the meeting ran over so that he was late for lunch his stomach churned and rumbled and he felt very anxious, and if the room became particularly hot he would have problems.

Desmond was able to write these observations down and work out ways of improving the way he dealt with them, but first of all he learned to sit comfortably in the meeting, near to the door if he had to. He learned to concentrate on slowing his breathing and physically relaxing so that he could get through the first ten minutes which were always the worst. He learned to notice when he was getting tense and to deal with that before it got too bad, and he became more aware of the things that started that tension off. Was it something that had been said? Was it hunger pangs, or the fact that when he was hungry his salivary glands produced saliva? Had he begun to sweat, and had his autonomic nervous system interpreted this prickly feeling in the back of his neck as the start of a panic attack? He relaxed away his fears.

If he had been in the audience at a big meeting and not skilled in the art of relaxation he could have done what a friend of mine used to do. My friend would assume an expression of intense interest and simply try to go to sleep. He hoped that he would not succeed and actually fall asleep in public, and fortunately he never did, but he did manage to relax. Indeed he had discovered the art of relaxation without being aware of it.

Your own problems

You have to think about your own problems in the sort of way that Desmond was taught to think about his. It isn't too difficult once you get the idea. Desmond's problems were important because they involved his job, but that gave him the advantage of having to sort them out as quickly as possible. He had every incentive possible to get on with them. Not every problem is like that. Some difficult situations can be avoided, and there is a temptation to ignore the problem. Let's say that you have a problem going to the cinema or theatre because you feel panicky there. You may find that the big screen makes you feel dizzy and that the sound is intimidating. You might find that concerts or the theatre are difficult because of the formal atmosphere or the crowds. Of course you can avoid these places, but if you do your life is diminished and you feel that you are a less complete person.

The very fact that you can avoid a difficult place, or avoid an animal which produces uncomfortable symptoms, is part of the problem. If you can avoid a situation you will do so because that is human nature, but you will hate yourself for doing so, and as well as that your life will be restricted as a result. Is it worth making the effort to take on your problem? Only you will know, but why shouldn't you lead a full and complete life if it is possible to do so? If you are young, going to the cinema is a necessary part of your social life, and you need your social life if you are to make friends. Simple social situations can be important for the development of a normal life.

Make the effort

It is easy to avoid some situations, but for the sake of your self-confidence and self-esteem, it is surely worth making the effort. You may have special difficulties to overcome. One is that you may not be able to practise your difficult situation every day. It may be hard to work out a system of situations of increasing difficulty which will help you to progress as will be described in a later chapter, but then who said life was easy? Finding ways of dealing with your problem is part of the fun.

Your anxiety in some situations may be holding you back more than you think. You may have been making excuses to yourself for not doing some things which you would like to do, but feel unable to do because of a particular anxiety. It might be worth taking stock—maybe with the help of paper and pencil again. You know what your symptoms are. You know what situations make them worse, but how does that affect your life? What invitation have you turned down recently? What people have you not met that you would have wanted to meet? Have you avoided *anything* because of your anxiety, even very indirectly?

If the answer to any of these questions is yes, then you have little choice if you are to live a full and complete life other than to take on your anxiety and banish it. You know what your task is and how to go about it, and in later chapters you will learn more. For now I would encourage you to make the decision that you are going to do it. This takes courage, but it is worth it. Choose a problem which isn't too difficult—something you can reasonably manage. It might be the cinema at a quiet time. It has to be something only a little bit difficult, and you should have practised your relaxation and breathing exercises. You must have a reasonable hope of success because you don't want to be discouraged by failure, so choose a situation which is just a little bit threatening, something you can almost manage.

You need your courage now. Remember that you are going, say to the cinema, not hoping that you won't get your symptoms, but rather hoping that you will get them so that you will have the chance of using your relaxation techniques to control them. Confidence in your ability to control your symptoms will only come if you have had the chance to use your skills, and to demonstrate to yourself that you *can* do it.

It is only when you know that you can control your worst symptoms in your worst situations that you will have the confidence to banish your anxiety.

Only then will your symptoms fade into insignificance and eventually disappear altogether. It is this catharsis which ends anxiety, and it is your goal. You can see that it takes time and effort to learn to deal with your problems, and there are no short cuts. When you have mastered one situation you have to go on to the next, more difficult situation and apply the lessons you have learned. It does get easier as you become more proficient, and as you learn more about yourself and the workings of your body you will want to do more.

Relaxation is the key to much of this, not because there is any magic in relaxation itself, but because it gives you back some control over your body and so gives you the confidence that you can manage your physical problems if they seem to be getting out of control. This breaks the cycle where fear of your symptoms makes them worse, and it gives you a new attitude to your anxiety. You are able to use your relaxation not only to treat your symptoms, but also to identify those symptoms when they happen, and as early as possible. It demystifies your anxiety and allows you to look around for other ways of helping yourself, and there are many.

REMEMBER:

- It is worth taking on your problems, even if you can avoid them.
- Begin with situations you find only a bit difficult.
- You may still get your symptoms, but you should practise controlling them.
- Practise as often as you can.
- Always look for other ways of managing difficult situations.
- Keep at it. Keep working. Never give in to anxiety.

Chapter 8

Moving on

There are many ways of helping yourself. They are all common sense and down-to-earth because there is nothing extraordinary about your anxiety. Simple measures are not necessarily easy to put into effect however, nor are they necessarily obvious to the person who is suffering from the anxiety. You can be so wrapped up in your problem that you can't see any way out.

It isn't easy to keep working at your problems either, particularly if you don't have anyone to help you or encourage you. It's very easy to backslide, to find an excuse for not doing something and to carry on in the same old way. Many people who have been anxious for years have developed lifestyles which allow them to avoid difficult situations. They lead slightly limited lives and are prepared to put up with that in return for a comfortable life. This is a perfectly valid approach, but it has its drawbacks.

The main drawback is that your life is limited, that you never fulfil your potential, and that at the back of your mind there is the constant fear that you will someday have to confront the situation you find so difficult. For many people a limited life just isn't acceptable. They are ambitious and able and see no reason why they should be second best to others less able. People with high anxiety are often high achievers.

Desensitization

So far we have used our relaxation and other techniques to help us manage particular situations which occur in our everyday lives and cause us problems. We have used them for the easier situations so that we don't have failures and become disillusioned. But we want to do more than that. We want to banish our anxiety altogether, and that means tackling all the situations in which we feel anxious. In other words, we have to progress through a list of situations of increasing difficulty until we have mastered the worst possible situation we can imagine. This takes courage, but most of all it takes organization and, of course, that means a pencil and paper. You have to progress in slow stages, climbing the rungs of your ladder carefully, and making sure that you take one rung at a time and never move on until you are comfortable with the rung you are on.

I use the word desensitization, a medical term for a technique used to banish allergies. In many ways anxiety can be seen as a psychological allergy to a particular allergen, which is a substance or situation which produces a reaction. In both a real allergy, and a psychological allergy, the end result is a physical reaction.

If you are allergic to a substance it used to be commonplace to go through a procedure of desensitization, though this is now rarely used because of the potential dangers involved. If you are to be desensitized against a substance, say grass pollen, you are given an injection of a very dilute concentration of that substance. The next week you are given a more concentrated dose, and so on until the body doesn't respond to that substance. Your immune system has been desensitized because it has become used to the substance.

You can use the same approach to your anxiety. You can't tackle the worst situation you might have to face simply because it would be too difficult, so you have to find a situation which is only mildly threatening. That might be the corner shop for a woman who has panic attacks in the supermarket queue. For someone who is housebound by anxiety in the form of agoraphobia, it might be a walk to the end of the street and back. Choose a situation which is only mildly threatening and which you can practise often.

Now go to the other end of the scale and select the most difficult situation you might want to face. Make sure it is realistic and practical, and something you can practise. This is the end point of your scheme, the ultimate target. You might like to write down your first and last target, and then fill the gap in between with the steps along the way, using four or five targets of increasing difficulty leading up to your most difficult target.

Do this realistically. Make sure that the targets are reasonable and attainable, and be sure that you are prepared to work at them. Make sure that your last target is something that you really want to do so that you have plenty of incentive. This is the way forward, and the only way forward, so perhaps we should look at how some other people have handled their particular problems.

Catherine

Catherine was a lady of 35 years who was happily married with two young children. I had seen her many times with the children when she brought them with the usual childhood illnesses. She had always seemed to be a competent, able person, so I was surprised when she came to see me on her own account and told me about her problems.

She had been experiencing an increasing sense of desperation over the preceding weeks, and she didn't really know why. Everything in her life seemed to be satisfactory. She loved her husband and her children, she had no financial problems, and everything in her particular garden was as good as it could be. Her feeling of unease seemed to have come from within herself.

So what was the problem? Catherine felt comfortable and happy as long as she stayed in her own house, but if she went out, things began to go wrong. Going out made her feel panicky, and if she went to the supermarket, which she used to do twice a week, she became quite ill. She couldn't say in what way she felt ill, but on several occasions recently she had had to abandon her trolley and run from the store. Now she felt that she couldn't go back. She couldn't understand what had happened, and she had no idea what she could do about it.

We talked for a long time. Her problems were explained, and as we talked her visible tension relaxed. Her problems seemed more logical then she had believed, and best of all, there seemed to be an answer to them. She went away for a week to keep a diary and to practise relaxation exercises. Just understanding her problem made her feel better.

A week later Catherine came back with her diary. It seemed that she felt panicky in many situations, visiting family and friends, even going for a walk. There was no doubt whatsoever though, that her worst problem was the supermarket. When asked, that was the situation she most wanted to manage. But here lay a problem. We have said that you shouldn't tackle a problem which is too difficult, you shouldn't risk defeat and disappointment. What is the way forward?

A plan of action

Catherine was advised that she would have to proceed in small steps. She had to make a list of situations of increasing difficulty, and she used her diary to sort out her campaign.

Plan of Campaign

Smith's corner shop (quiet time)

Corner shop (busy)

Montgomery's store

Local post office

Supermarket (Thursday morning—quiet)

Supermarket (busy—with Jim)

Supermarket (busy—alone)

Catherine's plan of campaign

We sat down together and came up with the above. Catherine agreed to start at stage one and take things slowly, gaining control of her symptoms and becoming comfortable with one situation before going on to the next. To her surprise, she found that it worked, and what is more, as soon as she started to tackle her problem she began to feel better so that there was an immediate pay-off. Life turned round for Catherine quite soon after her visit to my surgery.

You can do the same thing for yourself. Make out your own list. Work out how you are going to tackle each of your tasks so that you have a coherent plan of action, and then get on with it. But how do you make sure that you stick to your plan? There is only one way and that is to write it all down and record your progress at the time. Practise every day and record how you feel. It might help to record the severity of your symptoms in numerical form, giving a score from one to five to each symptom depending upon how severe it is at any given time. Your target diary might look like this:

	TARGET: Montgomery's Shop
MONDAY	Went to shop 10.30 a.m. Waited outside. *Felt shaky.* 3 Better on finding shop empty. Bought milk. *Tremor.* 4
TUESDAY	Felt *sick* going down road. 3 Went straight in. *Shaky.* 3 Small queue. *Dizzy.* 4

Target Diary

If you enjoy keeping records you can make it more effective by drawing a graph. Add up the scores at the end of the week and draw a graph of the severity against time, and with luck you will see a decline in the severity of your symptoms. These ploys are necessary because progress is slow and it can be disheartening, so involve someone else in your plans if you can. Make sure that your partner, relative or friend knows what you are doing and is able to give you encouragement and support. Being anxious is lonely and miserable, and it is easy to become discouraged, so make out a plan and stick to it.

The situation hierarchy

This plan of campaign may not be as easy to construct as you might think, or as it was for Catherine. Life doesn't always fit into the slots we would like it to. You may have generalized anxiety which isn't particularly worse in one situation, and often you can't practise the things you find difficult every day. It may not be easy to set up a list of situations of increasing difficulty, so you may need an alternative approach.

It may not be situations which make you anxious. It may be other things such as high winds or thunder, or you may find boats or planes a cause of anxiety. It might be animals which make you feel anxious, and again it isn't easy to construct a hierarchy for these. You can't always arrange to face a dog, cat, hen or cow every day of the week, just as you can't arrange for there to be thunder just when you want it. If you are to tackle these difficult situations you have to use your ingenuity. You can always start with your imagination, and you can use your relaxation sessions to recreate the problem you want to desensitize yourself to. Remember that you must always choose something which is only slightly threatening so that you can control your symptoms in that situation, and so that you have room to increase the difficulty of the problem. Someone I know had this sort of problem.

Andrew

Andrew was a young man who hadn't reached his twentieth birthday when he first told me about his problem. Some people have difficulty deciding what causes their symptoms, but Andrew had no such dilemma. He had a straight phobia. His problem is a common one, but he felt that he was the only one to suffer from it. Quite simply, Andrew had a dog phobia.

Andrew went rigid when he saw a dog, any dog, anywhere. He simply froze. He couldn't continue on his way. He had all the symptoms you might guess he would have when he met a dog, and it was affecting his life. Why?

Well, you or I might be able to avoid dogs in our everyday lives, but Andrew came from farming stock, and he had begun work as an agricultural company rep. He had to go into farmyards and he had to talk to farmers, and farmers have dogs. If there was a dog in the yard, Andrew had to stay in his car and make his excuses. He knew that he wouldn't keep his job that way.

Almost as bad for Andrew was the fact that he made his social life in the farming community, so that if he went to any of his friends' houses, or if he was to take a girl out, he would have to stay in his car until the dog was safely locked up. Clearly the situation was intolerable. He wanted help, but how could he arrange a hierarchy of situations of increasing difficulty? Dogs aren't that easy to organize for the purposes of desensitization. Still, Andrew was highly motivated to do something about his problem, and he had all the insight he needed. All that had to be added was the plan of action.

Andrew learned deep relaxation and practised it until he could really do it. His dedication and progress were exemplary. Then he commenced on a desensitization programme which began by using his imagination, and at the end used real dogs, dogs belonging to friends of his which he knew were reasonably quiet. He made this his plan of action.

You can be *too* imaginative. One patient of mine, a middle-aged man who became anxious on buses, began by relaxing in his home and imagining the problems he might have on his journey. When he came back to see me after a week I asked him how he had got on. He told me that it had been terrible. His bus journey had been a nightmare. He had managed the first few stops very well, but then a crowd of students had got on and the bus had rapidly filled up. By the time he had got to the city centre he was feeling terrible, and then he had had a panic attack and the bus driver had stopped the bus and sent for an ambulance. It had been a disaster.

I initially thought that the man had actually made the real journey, but he had only made it in his imagination. He should have made a relaxed comfortable journey, stopping and relaxing when he felt tense, but it is imagination had taken over and his imaginary journey had been worse than any real journey could ever have been. We had to start over again from scratch. My patient may have overdone his imaginary journey, but his experience illustrates the point that you can do a lot with your imagination.

You will have to be ingenious. If you have anxiety in a lift you must eventually practise lifts. There are plenty of lifts around, so choose one at a quiet time and go up one floor, then go up two floors the next day and so forth, perhaps going at a busier and busier time.

Avoid testing yourself. Don't say to yourself that you might just try a down-town supermarket because you happen to be passing. You are trying to re-educate your autonomic nervous system by benefiting from your successes. You don't want failures or setbacks. Progress slowly, one step at a time, and avoid setting unattainable targets. Of course you will have failures and setbacks, but not disasters.

If you have a setback don't despair. You never go back to the beginning again. If you have to leave a meeting or the theatre because you feel panicky don't feel that you have let yourself down. Everyone has their bad days and you will have yours. You may have made your hierarchy too difficult, or there may be other problems with your life which are creating pressure at that time. If you have a failure just go back a stage and continue with your programme.

Difficult problems

There may be situations you cannot rehearse. There are the 'one-off' situations which you won't meet again, or will only meet as infrequently as once a year. Such a situation might be flying in an aircraft, something you only do once a year, or it might be the prize-giving if you are a teacher, or the presidential address at the bowling club. You may cope very well with the everyday events of your life, but you still have your threshold of anxiety, your mental equivalent of the charging bull.

These things are talked about more and more openly these days. There are self-help groups for anxious people, and self-help groups for particular situations such as flying. Some psychologists will take classes in particular aspects of life which many people find difficult, but if you do find yourself in a situation where you feel panicky you should know by now what to do. If you are avoiding a difficult situation such as taking a holiday abroad, you should know what to do. You should make your plans and go. You now have ways of dealing with the panicky feeling you may experience, and you know that your symptoms can do you no harm. You shouldn't be leading a limited life through fear of what might happen, or fear of the symptoms you might experience. How can you manage these difficult situations?

Let's take flying. No one is going to argue about a fear of flying because it is so common. Many a 'high-flying' business executive can only manage to fly because he has taken a few whiskies in the departure lounge. It may be worse for you, but it is a matter of degree. You may experience dreadful symptoms in an aircraft, so bad that you think you are going to die. The entire experience may be so bad that you think you will never be able to face it. It may have limited your life and that of your family for years.

The same may be true of other situations. You may have avoided accepting an official position in a club or society because of a difficulty with public speaking, and worse than that you may have avoided promotion at work, or avoided changing your job because of a particular anxiety. That is tragic, because you are as able as anyone else, and it is only one small problem which is keeping you back. With all of these particular difficulties you have to ask yourself if you really want to do something about it, if you really want to make the effort. Do you want to take the family on a continental holiday? Do you want to make the presidential address? If the answer is yes then you should do something about it.

Relaxation and desensitization can only do so much, but even so they are worth doing, using all the techniques we have already talked about, and some we are going to talk about in the next chapter. If you are going to use your imagination make your practice sessions as realistic as possible. Don't be embarrassed because this is serious business. Use a picture of an aircraft, or the recording of a speech, any tricks which will make your rehearsal more realistic. Practise in your imagination as often as you can.

Actual rehearsal may be impossible, but there are things that can be done. You may not be able to fly in an aircraft, but flying is only part of the experience of travelling. You can go to the airport months before you will have to fly. You can go and have a cup of coffee and watch the planes. You can look at the queues at the check-ins, and you can stand in the airport building breathing quietly and relaxing so that the actual experience of arriving at the terminal and checking in is as familiar and easy as possible.

You can do the same thing before a lecture. You can go to the lecture theatre or the hotel and just sit quietly, absorbing the atmosphere. You can go as often as you need to, but of course that is only a partial help. Eventually there is the event itself. You have to take that on with a full frontal assault and you know it won't be easy. But will it be as difficult as you anticipate?

What if...?

Anticipation is often the worst part of any event. It takes the form of the 'what if' syndrome. What if I shout out? What if I make a fool of myself? What if I faint? What if I can't breathe? What if . . . almost anything. There's an answer to the 'what if's'. It's the *'what if . . . so what?'* answer. Nothing will happen of course, but if it does, does it matter? If you panic and have to leave, does it matter? Would anyone notice, or would they care? Surely people leave meetings all the time, often to go to the toilet or to get a breath of air.

What if something happens on an aircraft? If you are on an aircraft you may feel dreadful, but you can't get off and this is a mixed blessing. It may make you feel closed in and panicky, but when you are there all you can do is to wait for the flight to be over. What can happen? What if you faint in a public place? Well, people faint all the time and no one thinks that it is extraordinary. What if you dry up during a speech? People do so all the time. You pause, sort yourself out, and carry on.

Keeping at it

If you are to succeed in banishing your anxiety you have to devise ways of keeping up the momentum. It's much too easy to make excuses for not doing something. It's like going on a diet to lose weight, or a New Year's resolution to take more exercise. If you are to lose weight the first thing a dietitian will do is to give you a chart on which to record your hopefully decreasing weight so that you have a visual record of just what is happening. You might even be able to draw a graph of your weight loss.

Other systems will use forfeits if you don't lose the required amount of weight, or some commercial diet plans will charge you so much for their product that you will feel obliged to do what is required. The same approach is required if you are to banish your anxiety. You must do something to keep you at it. One approach is to keep a record of your relaxation sessions in your diary, and to set targets for the situations you are mastering. If you are to succeed with this desensitization, you have to keep at it using all the powers at your disposal. In many ways this is the most difficult thing of all to do. It's easy to make plans. It's putting them into effect which is difficult.

Decatastrophizing

This is an extention of the 'what if' scenario. If you really want to know what will result if something happens, take it to its logical conclusion. What if happen if I feel dizzy? I might faint. What will happen if I faint? Someone will help me to go outside. What will people think? People will just think that I have fainted, won't they? And people will say to each other, 'That person fainted, but then it was very hot, wasn't it?' People always rationalize things. If you ask yourself 'what if' over and over again you will come to the worst scenario that could possibly happen, the worst personal catastrophe possible.

What happens if you are on an aircraft and you panic? You will feel uncomfortable. You will sweat. You will get a tremor. What if you faint? Well, you faint. What if someone notices? People are always nervous on aircraft, they would think nothing of it. What if you make a scene and cry out? The air host or hostess will come and help you. None of this is very nice, but it isn't the end of the world, not compared with divorce, illness, or the loss of a job. The point is that even if the worst possible thing happened to you in any situation, what might result would probably be social embarrassment. You may think this a terrible thing, but there *are* worse catastrophes.

We have gone to great lengths to decide that anxiety is normal, or at worst an exaggeration of something that is normal. Normal things can do you no real harm.

Conforming

We can agree that increased anxiety is a common complaint, yet you will have noticed that public events aren't constantly disrupted by people fainting, running out, being sick or wetting themselves or anything like that. In any given situation there will be dozens, if not hundreds of people who are to some extent anxious. Despite this, an air hostess told me recently that she had never seen a passenger having an obvious panic attack, and a radio presenter once told me that he had never had an interviewee clam up on the air. That seems amazing to me, but it is true. Did it ever strike you that there might be a reason for it?

Humans are communal animals. We live in a group, and we have a strong instinct to conform. It is a very strong instinct, part of our social development. It's easy to imagine catastrophe in advance of what happens, but it rarely occurs when the time comes. Then the situation is different. Then you have an audience, a crowd, and colleagues, and as a result you conform, no matter how bad you feel. You can be confident that you and your body will do your best to conform. It'll be all right on the night.

Other people will notice

No they won't. People avoid staring at each other. They are too involved with themselves. If they are talking to you they will be thinking of whatever clever thing they are going to say next and probably aren't even listening to you. You aren't as conspicuous as you feel. No one will notice you unless you make them do so. People who want to be noticed have to go to bizarre lengths to make themselves conspicuous.

Relax, breathe slowly and move slowly, stay quiet and nothing will happen. But you want to be able to do more than that. You want to be a success in public, to be able to perform, to do yourself justice. Next we will consider ways of achieving that.

REMEMBER:

- You can desensitize yourself to difficult situations.
- You can control difficult situations.
- Conforming means that things will be better on the night than you expect.
- People don't notice that you are anxious.
- The worst doesn't happen.

Chapter 9

Other ways of helping yourself

It may have become apparent that many people suffering from excessive anxiety lack confidence. It isn't a matter of just saying they lack self-confidence because that is a blanket term which suggests that they lack confidence in all of themselves, and that isn't true. Anxious people have lost confidence in some aspects of their lives or in some of their abilities. They may still be confident for example, about their ability to do their jobs, and they will know that they are more able than many people who progress higher and faster than they do because those people seem more confident, or more brash. Confidence can seem to be more important than ability. Anxious people can often lose confidence.

It can also be the other way round. It may well be that you are anxious because you have lost confidence in one small aspect of your life. It may be a small part of your life but of course it may be an important part, such as driving a car or meeting people. It would be a pity if your work prospects, social life or indeed any aspect of your life was limited by some apparent quirk in your make-up which tends to make you a little more anxious in some specific situations. Anxiety and lack of confidence are linked:

- Anxiety . . . physical problems in some situations . . . worry about performance . . . loss of confidence . . . loss of ambition.
- Loss of ambition . . . loss of confidence . . . worry about performance . . . physical problems in some situations . . . Anxiety.

Increased anxiety is a wheel that goes round both ways. Most of the time all you seem able to do is to make things worse. So far we have concentrated upon breaking the cycle by learning to control the physical problems which anxiety produces using relaxation and thus increasing confidence in performance. Are there any other ways we can increase confidence, because if we can it will have the same effect and reduce our anxiety proportionally. Let's look at the wheel of anxiety (page opposite) and see what we can do.

Reorganization

We have already agreed that avoiding situations only makes things worse. The more you avoid doing something the more difficult it is to do it, and at the end of the day you can't avoid all of the situations all of the time. You certainly shouldn't avoid situations unless they are part of your desensitization plan.

It is important to realize that you may be avoiding some situations without realizing that you are doing it. You can be avoiding small situations, such as meeting a particular person in the corridor, by having sandwiches in your room at work instead of going to the cafeteria. Or you may just find excuses for not going to the cinema with friends or family. You may have decided that you prefer having holidays at home because you really don't like the travelling, when in fact you would love to travel abroad and it's your flying anxiety which keeps you at home.

You shouldn't avoid situations, you should find ways of dealing with them and still manage to do what you would really like to do. Reorganizing parts of your activities so that you can still do them is a form of avoidance, but if it is temporary it is probably acceptable. It is better to arrange to sit at the end of the row at the theatre than never to go to the theatre at all. It is better to sit near an exit in a stadium than to always watch on television.

The problem with this approach is that you spend your entire life hoping that you won't be put into a position which you will find threatening. You might go to the theatre with friends and find that you can't sit at the end of a row, and then you start to panic. Worse than that, every time you go out you worry in case you won't be able to organize the event you are going to to your own advantage and that you will get into a situation you won't be able to manage.

You can't predict every situation. You can't always know if the

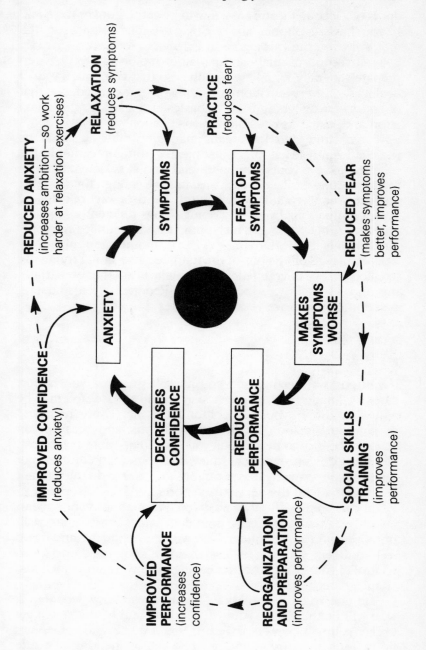

doors of a lecture theatre are going to be at the front or the back. If you have a phobia about driving under bridges on the motorway you can't always be sure that your route won't include a small section of dual carriageway or motorway. You have to prepare generally for all eventualities so that you have a way of dealing with every situation, including the unexpected, and that of course means going back to basics and starting with relaxation and, as far as possible, desensitization.

Reorganizing your life means managing difficult situations more efficiently. That might just mean getting up earlier in the morning to give yourself time to relax and slow down, or to go to the meeting earlier so that you can have enough time to relax and get your adrenalin under control. Think of ways of defusing anxious situations by simply doing things differently.

There are many things which pump up adrenalin for everyone. Arriving late is one. Driving too fast is another. You might buy a paper to read on the bus or the train because sitting trying not to catch the eye of your fellow passengers is another embarrassing and adrenalin-producing factor. Reorganization and preparation can improve your confidence.

Preparation

If you go to a meeting and you haven't prepared your report carefully enough you will obviously feel ill at ease. You may be a little cavalier in your preparation for events. Everyone has to do some preparation for difficult situations, and because you have a tendency to be anxious you have to do more than most. You must do your research, know that you are in command of the situation as much as you can be. You have to do the relevant reading and read the necessary reports.

You can prepare in other ways too. What about your appearance? You want to project a confident image by dressing well, because if you look confident you will feel confident, and if you feel confident you will be less anxious. Look good and be in control of your part of the proceedings and you stand much less chance of feeling anxious.

Find out what the event is all about. If you know where it is, who will be there, how you will get there and how you will get home, you will be well armed. If you are going to someone's house for a meal, try to find out who will be there, and be sure that you know what sort of event it will be. Will it just be a light supper, or a full meal, and how long might you have to stay?

Eating is important, because if you are hungry you will feel anxious, and eating in public can be tricky for some very anxious people. Try to get it right. Preparation isn't hugely important because you don't want to go through life trying to prejudge every situation, to work out all the angles. That isn't practical because you can get it wrong and end up feeling even more anxious, but you should at least do what other people do, and be as prepared as the average person would be. Be determined to enjoy yourself.

This applies to all kinds of things from speaking engagements to travelling by train, boat or plane. Find out what is required of you, what you will have to take with you, what you will have to know. Don't leave things to the last moment. Be one step ahead of the game, because that is where confidence comes from. Confident people tend to be well prepared.

The experts

You can learn a lot from your own experience of life, by the things that happen to you and by watching others. You can also learn from the experts, and why not? They have learned by watching the people who have gone before them.

I had to organize a national conference for an association of doctors once and I found it a daunting experience. One of the things I had to do was to brief the president-elect about the history and organization of the association and tell him what his duties would be during the conference and later during his year in office. He was a venerable medical man with a national reputation, and I was somewhat in awe of him.

I met him first at his house where we had an informal conversation, but I noticed that he made notes. He wanted to know a lot about the association, and in subsequent meetings we went over the details of all that was expected of him, often recapping things we had covered before. He entered all timings in a big diary and nothing was missed. I have to admit that I got a little fed up with the constant rehearsal of the coming events, but then I wasn't very experienced in these matters.

I realized what all the meetings had been about the evening before the conference when he held a reception at his house for the organizing committee. I was there in advance of the members and was surprised to discover that this eminent medic was nervous. I just hadn't expected it. What happened next was an even greater surprise.

As the committee members began to arrive I found that our president-elect knew them by name, which was more than I did, and he knew a great deal about each of them. Now I hadn't told him these details, so he must have done some more research on his own. He had anecdotes about the hospitals and medical schools they had come from, and in short he carried the evening like the true professional he was. His research and his technique were what had made him the famous man he was, and it had helped him to overcome the natural anxiety which most people feel before an important event.

The president-elect carried the conference better than anyone else there. It was an object lesson for me on just how to conduct oneself on such an occasion, but the same rules apply to any event at which one has to officiate or even attend. You don't want to be a bore, but if you do want to impress, prepare.

Remember that people take you as they find you, or rather as what you seem to be, and the world is full of good actors. Don't try to pretend to be something that you aren't, but if you know that you look confident, you will feel confident, and if you feel confident you will be less anxious.

Social skills

If you find some social situations difficult it may be that you have forgotten, or perhaps never fully developed, the relevant social skills. These skills are taken for granted by many people who have no difficulty meeting others, saying the right thing at the right time, knowing when to shake hands and how much eye contact to make, but many people in all walks of life find these things difficult. These skills are like any other skills, they can be learned, and when you have learned the correct skills you will be more confident in company—and confidence reduces anxiety.

It may be that this sort of thing doesn't come easy to you. If you tend to be shy or diffident you can feel awkward and tentative in the company of others, and if that is the case it is well worth while doing something about it, and there are things that you can do. We can all improve our social skills.

Preparation and practice can again be useful. No salesman would go to see a client if he couldn't remember his client's name and a few details about his particular interests, both social and professional. The salesman can't rely on his memory if he has a large number of clients, so what does he do? Many salesmen or people in a similar occupation will keep a short file on their customers, and will refer to it in the car just before they pay their client a visit. They may have made a few notes about subjects discussed at their last meeting, including details of the customer's family and hobbies. That way they are immediately in control of the situation and feel confident.

Some doctors will do the same sort of thing, making an *aide-mémoire* so that they can give the impression that they remember their patient better than they perhaps do. A few people will keep notes or a diary of people they may come in contact with so that they can do a little research before a social event or a meeting if they know who is going to be there. It isn't really cheating, more a way of giving yourself confidence because if you tend to be anxious, you also tend to be preoccupied with your own problems in public and are more likely to forget names and details.

Names

If you forget personal details about people, what about names? How can you remember names? How do other people remember names? It's a social skill which can be learned. Next time you are introduced to someone in a formal or work situation notice how many times he says your name. He will repeat it when you are introduced, and if there is an ensuing conversation he will say your name as often as he can, thus engraving it on his memory.

You could do the same thing, but if at the end of the day you really can't remember names it is probably better to admit the fact, tell people you can't remember names, and just get on with the evening.

Eye contact

Many people feel embarrassed in company. They have trouble interacting with others and part of the difficulty may be that they don't know how much eye contact they should make. It's part of being, literally, self-conscious. If it doesn't come naturally it is something you can learn. The problem is that if you make too much eye contact you may seem to be staring, and that signals aggression to the person you are talking to. If you make too little eye contact you may seem disinterested. If you can master these details of social intercourse you will feel more confident and therefore less anxious.

There is only one way to go about doing that, and that is to practise in front of the mirror by yourself. Do it often, do it in your imagination with the people you are going to be with until you are comfortable, and then deliberately practise your eye contact technique in the real situation.

Talking

Do you talk too much? Do you talk too loudly, or do you sit in a corner and say nothing? There is a knack to everything, and it is a knack you can learn. If you have to say a few words to the assembled company in the course of the evening or of the meeting, practise with a tape recorder so that you know what your voice sounds like. That way it won't be a surprise when you hear yourself speaking in public.

If you want to learn social competence, and that is what this is all about, watch and listen to others. Find someone who is socially adept and see how he or she does it. You don't have to like or want to be like the person, but you do want to pick up tips. See how others do it and then develop your own style.

The same applies to talking to the opposite sex in a social situation. It's better to talk too little than too much because someone who is quiet is often thought to be wise. You don't want to copy someone else because then you would just sound false, but you can learn social skills by watching and listening, and then practising these skills, first at home, and then in 'real life'.

Younger people

Developing social skills is particularly relevant for young people. Those of us who are older have often developed ploys for dealing with social situations, though of course we can still improve our performance. Younger people often feel gauche and awkward, and frequently self-conscious. Unlike many older people, they really care what other people think about them, particularly if those people are of the opposite sex. Appearance and sexual attractiveness are very important, and it is very difficult to be at one's best if one is anxious.

The anxiety which younger people feel may be related to these very factors, about performance in public, about how they appear to others, and about how competent they may be in dealing with the advances and expectations of the opposite sex. No discussion of anxiety would be complete without a consideration of these problems which are as old as time, and still as important today as ever. Anxiety about appearance and performance in public may be linked with fears and anxieties about performance in private, about sexual adequacy and attractiveness, about all sorts of personal things which you might not want to discuss or maybe even acknowledge.

Life isn't easy for young people. There are many things to face up to and many new skills to master. If you are anxious about your abilities it is hard to feel confident, and you can get stuck on the downward spiral.

Michael

Michael was 17 years of age and still at school when he first came to see me. He came, not because of any physical illness, but because of his extreme unhappiness. I have no idea what his expectations were or how he thought I might be able to help. He really just wanted to talk to someone about his problems, and I was the only person available.

At first it was hard for me to believe that Michael had any problems. He was tall, good-looking and seemed competent and able in every way. He was very bright and had a place at university, but he wasn't happy. We had quite a long talk and some things emerged from our conversation. I had wondered at first if he had problems with his sexuality, but that wasn't it. He had difficulty identifying his problems himself, but it seemed that he was uncomfortable and uneasy in many social situations, and that his life was limited as a result. As he couldn't manage social encounters very well, he didn't make friends easily, and he did not have a girlfriend.

That was as far as Michael could go about his problems, and he was apologetic about discussing his difficulties at all, and in a way he was right, compared with other people who had serious medical conditions he was very lucky. Yet he wasn't happy, and his problems were interfering with his life in a major way so that he was becoming a social invalid. He certainly needed help.

Michael was keen to solve his problems and to cooperate as best he could. How did he begin? He was asked to write about his problems so that both he and I could be more precise about just what was going on. When he had done this it became clear that much of the misery in his life came down to one phobia, a typical social phobia. Michael got unpleasant symptoms in certain situations. If the atmosphere in any place became tense at all, he became uncomfortable, sweaty and dizzy. He was worse in crowded places, even pubs, and the cinema, theatre and concerts were a nightmare. If Michael had been a recluse none of this would have mattered, but he wasn't a recluse—he had a life to lead, people to meet, interviews to go to and a degree to get. All this seemed impossible to Michael and he was in despair.

If Michael went to a concert he would dread the slow movement or the quiet song, or the emotional scene in a play. In those situations he would start to swallow desperately, feeling that he was choking. That was something which came from his diary. At a party his pulse would race and he would feel sweaty so that when he was talking to a girl he almost couldn't speak, and when he did speak he talked gibberish. He never did himself justice and he had lost all confidence in himself and his abilities. He was on the downward spiral.

He had nearly hit the bottom of his spiral. He had developed the idea that there was something physically wrong with him, and his anxiety had begun to spill over into a nightmare of physical symptoms and worry. He felt that his worry was unnecessary, but he couldn't stop worrying. He had begun to think that he had a sexually transmitted disease. All this emerged from discussions about his diary, but his secret fears were really just the end result of his uncertainties about his own worth. He had no confidence in himself at all.

Michael followed what should be now a familiar path. He put to one side those things which he couldn't deal with, and that included some of his irrational ideas. He took an entirely practical approach, learned to relax and manage social situations better, and understood what was happening to him. He used all the techniques he could, including all those tricks which would help him to present himself in a more confident way in public so that he rapidly became more socially adequate. He had thought that he was going mad, and indeed his irrational ideas were disturbing, but I had been of the opinion from the beginning that they were secondary to his severe anxiety state, and I was right. As Michael's body relaxed, so did his mind, and the stresses produced by his anxiety disappeared.

Michael got better, became more confident, more relaxed, more in control. He had been just one side of the line which divides the comfortable state from the uncomfortable and he was able to cross over, but what he wanted most of all was a girlfriend to believe in him, and when he found one he at last fully believed in himself and put the uncertainties of the past behind him.

Make a start

No matter how bad things can seem, not matter how hopeless, no matter how long you have been anxious and what its spin-off effects may be, once you recognize the central problem and make a start on dealing with it, you will be surprised how quickly things can turn round. All you have to do is make a start.

REMEMBER:

- It is very difficult to be confident and anxious at the same time.
- Preparation helps you to feel confident—and so less anxious.
- You can improve your social skills.
- You can learn to project a confident image.

Chapter 10

Managing anxiety

The time has come to get out and about, to put into effect everything we have been talking about. There have been situations you have been avoiding, situations you have been hating, and parts of your life that haven't been fulfilled. There is no alternative in this life to simply living it, and living it to the full.

If you are an anxious person there is every chance that you have been doing everything but living your life to the full. Anxiety is like a dead weight which you drag around after you. It holds you back. It keeps you from fulfilling your potential. At its worst it can ruin your life. You can control anxiety, and you can manage difficult situations well enough for you to live your life more or less normally. That's worth working for.

We will have to use the skills we have already discussed, learned and practised. What we have to think about now is how we can apply these skills to our everyday lives. That is critical, and remember that you have to have the courage to actually go out and practise in the real world because you can only do so much at home. But first of all, what about the anxiety some people feel in their own homes? That is just one of the problems some people have consulted me about over the years.

At home

Some people, and they are usually women who work in the home, feel anxious when they are alone in the house. There is that moment when the door closes behind their husband or children, and they are alone and the feeling isn't pleasant. If you are a paid-up member of the anxiety club you will know that feeling, and it's worse if you are alone. There is no one to share it with, nothing but the all-pervading silence.

For some women it will be so bad that they will arrange for a relative, maybe their mother, to come round in the morning and spend the day with them just so that they won't be alone, or else they take the first opportunity they have to go out to the shops. Of course this means that they are avoiding being alone, and as a result they will always fear being alone. It is much better to take on the problem and start to spend part of the day by themselves using whatever techniques they can to help them.

We can all understand that uneasy feeling one gets when one is left alone, when the house goes quiet. It is an eerie sensation most of us are aware of, but for some people it goes that little bit further and triggers off the adrenalin reaction that every reader of this book knows so well and can sympathize with. We all know what it's like, and how important it is to deal with it firmly, using, in this case, relaxation and desensitization techniques, extending the time you spend alone by even minutes a day until you become more comfortable, more relaxed and less anxious.

Remember also the great maxim—*slow down*. Don't hoover the house furiously from end to end as a distraction from one's own internal machinations. This simply charges up your adrenalin, so do the opposite instead, slow down and relax.

Wind noise

It may not be the silence of the house which causes your autonomic nervous system to over-react. There may be a specific reason, such as high winds. Many people find wind disturbing and they become anxious in a storm, or thunder and lightning may make them anxious. Again it is obvious why these things can be disturbing. We have all been overawed by the power of the wind and felt the hackles on the back of our necks rise as the trees bend and the doors rattle. For some people that is the adrenalin trigger, the thing that fires off their autonomic nervous system and makes them feel panicky.

Anyone who has experienced anxiety will know that there is no need to be embarrassed about feeling anxious in this sort of situation. What is experienced by a few people is just an exaggeration of a reaction common to all of us and to many animals. Watch horses or cattle in a wind. We understand it, and we feel for those of us who have to go through that ordeal every time there is a storm.

Take the problem on, using your imagination first of all, and then tape recordings, pictures, and anything else which will make your practice feel more real.

Noise

It may not be the noise of the wind, it may be just noise, the noise children made by—or worse, teenagers—or the noise of a radio or television. Some people find that noise is intimidating, that it starts off their adrenalin reaction. They too have to identify their problem, decide that they want to do something about it, and then work out exactly how to go about controlling their anxiety.

In the case of noise practice isn't too difficult. You can always turn up a record player by degrees for the purposes of your practice sessions, giving yourself progressively more noise to deal with and you can practise by yourself, which helps. You could even use earphones. It isn't so easy to summon up thunder. Then it's up to your imagination when you do your relaxation sessions.

Visitors

Everyone's home is their castle, as we all know. But for some people their home is also their fortress, the place where they feel safe. They don't welcome intruders because it broaches that feeling of safety. Again we can all understand that feeling. It may be the arrival of a large deputation of the family calling on a Saturday, or for someone who is anxious it might just be a salesman calling at the door, but whatever it is it brings on the adrenalin reaction, or it might be the hyperventilation reaction because the effect is the same. It's the same reaction as always, just as unpleasant as in any situation, and just as controllable. The problem is arranging practice.

Again one can start with the imagination, working with relaxation exercises, and if it's a dinner party or a family gathering, plan, rehearse and practise. Prepare well in advance, but be prepared to be flexible. Use all your social skills to project that natural air of relaxed confidence so that you know that you don't look or sound anxious.

If entertaining has to be part of your life, start with small groups of friends and work up in small steps to the boss and his or her spouse. The basic methods of dealing with the scourge of anxiety are always the same because anxiety is always the same. The trick is to adapt them to your own particular problem.

The telephone

Having to speak on the telephone can be a nightmare for some people. We know why, because we have all felt apprehensive before phoning an important, prestigious or aggressive person. No wonder some people become anxious about phoning anyone, or nervous about receiving calls. Who knows who might be on the other end?

Using the phone is always worse if there are other people in the room listening to your end of the conversation. That turns your already difficult conversation into a performance. Practise by yourself, but whom can you phone? Well, how about the speaking clock, and if you want to progress on to more and more pushy people you could always phone and inquire about double-glazing or time-share holiday homes. You'll have no trouble practising there!

Going out

For many people their home is a sanctuary. Even the idea of going out can produce severe adrenalin-type symptoms, and if such people avoid going out because of the severity of their symptoms they become housebound and are then considered to be agoraphobic. That can be just as disabling as any physical illness. For an anxious person going out may not be easy.

You may be familiar with these feelings. You may know what it's like to wake up in the morning knowing that something is wrong, and wonder what it is. Then you remember—you have to go out to some social function that evening. That's why you're feeling sick and ill. Your body has remembered before you have, and it's complaining already, before you get out of bed. The event you have to go out to may not be very important. It might just be an evening with friends, or a visit to the cinema. It's not the importance of the event which matters, just the fact that you're going out.

Of course, it may not be an event at all. It may just be going down to the shops which gives you the adrenalin reaction. You may feel fine sitting in the house, but the moment you have to go out to do a little shopping your heart rate speeds up, you feel sweaty, your tummy churns and you might even have diarrhoea. It's all very unpleasant, and very familiar. What can you do about it?

We have discussed this problem before, and you know about relaxing, slowing down, giving yourself time and most of all, actually going out, even it it's only a walk round the block. It's worth asking yourself why you feel so anxious. What would happen if the worst thing you fear actually did occur? The answer is, not much. If you can accept that all of the unpleasant sensations you feel are just functional symptoms which can do you no harm, then you may be able to actually go out and just let them burn themselves out. That takes courage, but then you have courage.

Your symptoms are real, especially your bladder or bowel symptoms, but they are still just exaggerations of the normal. You won't get into embarrassing situations. The worst won't happen, but the only way to prove that to yourself is to actually go out, see what happens, see how well you can manage. That does take courage, but you really do have to go out, perhaps with company. Don't go too far. Work to a programme and don't test yourself, don't be too ambitious, but *go*—and keep going.

When you are out

Let's take the least stressful venture out-of-doors. What about a walk round the block? That shouldn't be too difficult, but for some people it is very difficult indeed. Let's assume that as you walk away from the house you start to feel more and more panicky. That is what you would expect to happen. What happens if you start to feel very panicky? Then you do what anxious people should do every time in this situation, ask yourself a question. Ask yourself what is happening. Is there a reason for the way you feel?

You may have walked round a corner and found yourself facing a cold wind which causes your muscles to tighten up and that may be something your body interprets as a panicky feeling. Remember that your autonomic (or automatic) nervous system has become very sensitive and over-reacts to any external stimulus. So you may be cold, or you may be hot, with that prickly feeling down your back, or you may have been rushing or overexcited and as a result be out of breath and breathing heavily. Again your body translates this physical sensation as the onset of panic and you begin to feel very uneasy. If you know the reason why you feel a certain way you can handle it.

Go out for short periods and often until you are comfortable going out and being out.

Going places

If you want to go somewhere using some kind of transport, that is a step up from just walking to the shops. It is a very positive thing to get on to a bus because it takes you away from the sanctuary of your own home very rapidly, involves all kinds of social skills, and has a feeling of inevitability and irreversibility about it. On a bus, or a train, or in a car, you are in a sense trapped, just as you are in a lift or on the underground or subway. A plane may seem the worst of all.

Buses and trains

Public transport of any sort can be a problem for anxious people because of the trapped feeling they get. Yet you aren't really trapped in a bus or on a train. You can always get off. You are actually sitting on a seat, a situation in which you can practise your relaxation and breathing. Of course there are crowds of other people, and they can get on or get off so things can be unpredictable and you don't know exactly what might happen. You are away, and still moving away, from your home which is your sanctuary, and something might happen. What if it did? It doesn't matter how many 'what if's' you may have—and even if you had the worst of all things, a panic attack, so what!

Prepare well in advance so that you at least know where you are going and how you are going to get there, and just get on with it. Take a book or a newspaper so that you don't have to stare at other people in the carriage. Remember that the anticipation is always worse than the event and there is every expectation that when you get started you will be carried along by the momentum of the event, so as long as you can get yourself on to the bus or train you will get to your destination. You will survive.

Flying

All this is particularly true of flying. Remember when I asked that air hostess I know how often she had to deal with panic

attacks or attacks of hyperventilation on an aircraft and she told
me that it was extremely rare? Well, almost everyone I know has
a flying phobia, and dreads the thought of flying. One would
expect that an air hostess would have to deal with the problems
this produces every day, but she doesn't. Why not?

Flying isn't pleasant for the anxious person. It can't be,
because it has all the ingredients we hate. It's closed in, you
really can't get off, and there's the chance of motion sickness and
a multitude of ways of making a fool of ourselves. *Yet we don't*.
The reason for this lies in the other aspects of commercial flying.
It is a formal experience, with it's own litany—the 'emergency
exits are at the front and at the rear, fasten your seat belts'
speech. If you can get on the aircraft there is great pressure to
conform and of course you have no option but to sit in your seat
no matter how bad you may feel, and there is no doubt that an
anxious person may feel quite bad. So will many others but you
can go by the general experience, which is that people who start
tend to finish, without mishap.

So don't worry about flying too much. Your worry and your
preparation should be aimed at getting you on to the aircraft,
because if you can get on, you will certainly get off at the other
end. If you have been avoiding flying, give it your earnest
consideration because you are missing a lot, and because you
can do it.

Cars

Some people have a car phobia, or a phobia related to driving.
Perhaps you feel that you can't drive under a high-tension power
cable, or drive under a motorway bridge, or drive on a motorway
at all. It may be speed, going over or under bridges or viaducts,
or driving in the outside lane of a dual carriageway. These things
can bother you as a driver or as a passenger, and they can make
travelling difficult.

It's not so bad if you are a passenger because you don't have
the responsibility for transporting others or keeping safe control
of the car, and you can use your relaxation and breathing
techniques. Even as a driver you can relax and breathe slowly.
As a driver you can't guarantee that you won't encounter the
situations which trigger your anxiety, and you may spend your
life in fear of meeting one at the wrong time and so putting
yourself and your passengers at risk. There is no guarantee that

you won't have a panic attack, and although it will do you no harm and you will still be able to control your car, it will affect your confidence and your concentration.

The only approach to this problem is to practise your difficult situations as often as you can using all the techniques you have learned to help you. Find a motorway bridge to drive under and do it over and over again, or practise driving on the motorway at a quiet time and over a short distance. In general you can drive slowly, carefully and defensively, and at the same time safely. It really means being a good, careful driver, considerate to others and with good anticipation. Practise in your imagination, and practise in real life every time you have the opportunity.

If you are a really unsafe driver of course you shouldn't drive at all as your insurance policy would be invalid. You have a legal duty to notify the DVLC if you have a medical condition which affects your driving, and that includes an anxiety state. If you did disclose that you had such a condition the Medical Officer at the DVLC in Swansea would consult your doctor and if the condition was thought to interfere with your driving your licence could be withheld and your insurance invalidated. However it is a matter of judgement whether you are unsafe or not and in many cases it is unlikely that the driver would be unsafe. Just the same, remember that you have a duty to others and to being a careful driver.

Cinema, theatres and concerts

Going out to some form of entertainment involves many difficult problems for the anxious person—going out, using transport, being in a crowd, and worst of all, sitting in the audience. None of it is easy. Still, it is an important part of our lives, too important a part to opt out of, so let's consider ways of making it easier.

Firstly, choose the venue for your debut carefully. Don't start with a classical music concert because formality is the enemy of the anxious person. Choose the cinema, or an informal concert which you could walk out of if you wanted to. If you are booking, perhaps you could get an end of row seat, but there are dangers in doing that. A friend of mine did that recently only to find on his arrival that the end of row seat he had booked was at the end of a row against a wall, thirty seats from the aisle and his mode of escape. He managed very well just the same.

If you are very anxious your discomfort may begin before you get up in the morning and get progressively worse as the day goes on, even if your evening out is only to the cinema. Do your relaxation exercises and whatever preparation you want well in advance, and resolve early that you are going to go, no matter what. No last minute excuses, not another night in front of the television and a feeling of failure.

What you are dreading is the simple act of sitting in the audience. You know what that's like, the feeling that you are conspicuous, the thought that you might make a fool of yourself by shouting out or something like that. Then there is the increasing heat, the sweating and the increasing muscle tension. After that the creeping feeling that starts from your toes, moves up your body and across your head until you know that you are going to have a panic attack. Your bladder may feel uncomfortable even though you have been to the toilet, or you might feel the need to keep swallowing. Every anxious person has had that and knows exactly what it is like, and how desperate it can feel— like slow-motion drowning. They also know that it can be overcome.

You really have to learn to live with that feeling, knowing that it can do you no harm. You come to expect it, almost to welcome it, because the more you can practise managing it by just sitting quietly and breathing slowly, the less severe it will be until you can banish it altogether. All public performances generate tension. No performer tries to produce a relaxed audience which will go to sleep, and that applies to magicians, singers, orchestras and comedians. Even the cinema has its tension, being dark, loud and disorientating.

Sitting in an audience is a good place to do some 'decatastrophizing'. If you do have to leave, so what? Would anybody notice? If they noticed, what would they think? Would it matter what they thought? If you fainted would it be the end of the world? No! Start going out, but go to something you can manage, and expect the worst. Use it as an exercise in controlling your symptoms, which really means relaxing your way through them. Know that they generally get better as the evening wears on. Know and believe that nothing serious can happen to you, and be determined to enjoy yourself. And surprise, surprise, you just might!

Social gatherings

Everyone is invited out to a social event of some sort at some time. It's hard to refuse, and anyway such gatherings are meant to be enjoyable. For an anxious person they can also be painful. There is the problem of arriving, meeting those already present, finding a seat sometimes in a small room, and then making conversation. There may be a meal involved, and eating in public has its own difficulties. And as the evening goes on it gets hotter and hotter.

These problems may be difficult for older people, but for the young they can be very difficult indeed. Parties are designed to help people to get to know each other, and if that 'getting to know' involves people of the opposite sex things can get very tense. There are all the overtones of whether you are looking your best, or sounding your best, or giving the right impression, and on top of all that the anxiety about your own sexual acceptability. It's uncharted territory, and for someone who is shy, it can create a lot of anxiety.

You don't know what is expected of you, how you should behave, or how you will be accepted. It's a learning process, and some people just opt out and sit in a corner feeling more and more excluded, more and more anxious. Going to social events, whether you are young or old, whether you are super-attractive or just ordinary, is all about confidence. We have talked a lot about confidence and social skills before, and parties and social events are the times you need them most.

There is one tip which might be of use. Don't ever assume that other people are more confident or more able than you are. Some people, of any age, may *seem* more confident, but they may just have better social skills, and underneath they are probably as anxious as you are. If you want to do a test, watch guests arriving at a party. See how they bluster, or say the wrong thing, or just look embarrassed. That's why drinks are used as a social lubricant—to put people at their ease. So it isn't just you who is anxious and flustered.

Brush up on your social skills in advance. Say little, look calm no matter what you feel like, and try to be yourself. Remember too that in this situation, like in any other situation, no one is watching you intently. They are much too concerned about the state of their digestion, or their headache, or what they are going to say to impress you next. After a conversation they probably couldn't describe your appearance accurately, so you aren't as conspicuous as you feel. Other people absorb the impression you choose to give, so work on that, and learn to be a good listener. People like to be listened to, so practise saying just enough.

Eating out

Eating out presents particular difficulties for an anxious person. It is a formal occasion, you are trapped in the restaurant, you are usually in company, and then there is the matter of the food. Before the meal you are hungry, and the smell of food makes your gastric juices run and your tummy rumble. Your blood sugar may be low, and overall you may not feel too well. Why do people enjoy eating out so much?

Eating out can be an enjoyable experience. If you know just what's going on in your internal workings you can manage the little difficulties which develop. Remember that when your tummy starts to rumble, and your saliva starts to flow, your easily arousable autonomic nervous system can interpret the sensation as the onset of panic and fire off a panic attack. You may well feel uncomfortable before the meal, over and above what you might expect to feel in the typical 'trapped' situation which anxious people find so difficult.

Try to anticipate your problems. Think your way through the evening, particularly the start of the evening during a relaxation session. Imagine the people who will be there and what they will be like and what they will say. Relax and practise your contribution to the evening, which will be to look calm and stay comfortable. Dress appropriately. Have something to eat before you leave the house, particularly if the meal may be delayed.

When you get to the hotel or restaurant, 'play yourself in' by taking stock of the situation. When you are anxious you tend to get flustered easily, so slow down and deliberately notice things about the decor. Slow down, really listen when people are introduced, repeating their names if necessary, and then be prepared to make conversation, which often means listening to the talkers. As you gain in confidence you will contribute more yourself.

The enjoyment of good food and good wine, and the company of good friends is worth working for, so do work on your problem both at home before the event, and also by relaxing, breathing slowly and anticipating problems during the event. Notice what happens to you physically and look for a good physical reason for your sensations. There is no reason why you shouldn't be able to dine out comfortably.

Ceremonies

We all have to go to weddings and funerals, to graduations as well as to all sorts of other ceremonies such as prize-givings. Often we don't *have* to go to these things, we *want* to go to them because they involve people we love and care about, and because they are part of our lives and our traditions. Just the same, they can cause a lot of trouble for an anxious person. Why?

During formal occasions we are expected to act in a particular way. And then if we have a major part to play we will be conspicuous, and we might even have to make a speech. Add to all this the emotion which is generated by the nature of the event itself. Many a mother and father of the bride will shed a few tears at their daughter's wedding. Then there is a meal, never easy. At a funeral there is sadness and mourning. No one wants to break down in public. At a school event there is pressure to conform for the sake of one's offspring, even though events involving children can be very emotional.

You don't have many opportunities to practise ceremonies. They don't happen too often, but the general rules apply. Preparation, relaxation, slowing down, rehearsal and practise. Anticipation is worse than the event itself, so concentrate on getting yourself there on time and in one piece. Ceremonies are formal, they have a form, so it's like getting on a plane. Once you get started you will coast along until you finish. Lie back and let it happen. Let the professionals who organize these events take care of the details, while you concentrate on enjoying the event. You will find it easier than you think. If you have to make a speech, make sure that you are well-prepared and that you have a few easy-to-read standby notes.

Anxiety in other places

There are many other places where anxiety can cause problems, far too many to mention. Every anxious person will have his or her own special problems or fears. Some will be very personal. Some may be about sexual problems involving relations with others, about some of your own thoughts and ideas, or about the sexual act itself. Many of these problems can be dealt with using the general principles we have already discussed. Some will be dealt with in specialist books. Or you might want to talk to an expert. For all the other bothersome day-to-day problems you can work out your own strategy, because you will be aware that the solution to all problems is much the same. It requires imagination, the ability to adapt the general principles, and an ability to stick to doing the exercises.

If you can't deal with your problems yourself, you may have to seek the help of others, and that is what we deal with next.

REMEMBER:

- The problems of anxiety are the same in all situations.
- The solutions are also universal.
- The anticipation is always worse than the event.
- Other people cope. So can you if you prepare properly.
- Have the courage to tackle difficult situations. They will be easier than you think, and more enjoyable.

Chapter 11

Help!

Anxiety can be anything from very mild to severe to almost disabling. It is always difficult to manage, and it always has the result of making the person who suffers its effects feel lonely and isolated. It isn't an easy thing to talk about, and you may have had the experience of trying to tell a friend about how you feel and being met with blank incomprehension. It isn't an easy thing for other people to understand.

Confiding

If you are fortunate enough to have someone who cares about you enough to want to make the effort to understand and to help you, then the situation is easier. Perhaps having read this book you understand your own situation better and can explain it to others in a way that they can understand. You can talk about an overactive nervous system, about the functions of your autonomic nervous system, about learned responses, about the adrenalin reaction and the problems of overbreathing.

Most of all you can explain how physical symptoms, sometimes severe physical symptoms, can result from psychological problems, and how this is a common and necessary part of nature. You might even give them this book to read in the hope that they will get some insight into your problems, and perhaps even into some problems of their own. You feel better if you have someone to talk to about your own difficulties, but don't expect too much from others. It is very difficult for someone else to really understand how powerful your symptoms can be. Don't bore people by talking about your symptoms too much, even though you really want them to understand. Have sympathy with their position. Be careful whom you choose as your confidant. Don't choose your employer, or the local gossip, or someone who might not understand and might betray your trust. That would be devastating.

You don't really want sympathy, you want understanding and help, and that's different. You have to be able to tell people what sort of help you want, and the help which you need most of all is the encouragement to keep working at the exercises which will ultimately allow you to banish your anxiety. Doing these exercises and tasks by yourself is frustrating and boring. You need someone with whom you can discuss your progress, and who will shout at you if you start to backslide. That has to be a special person.

If you don't have someone close to you, you will have to manage without. You can talk to friends, explaining some of your problems, but friends tend not to understand, particularly if they are young and lack the maturity to comprehend the full nature of your problems, but they can understand some of your difficulties, so tell them what they need to know if they are to help you with your everyday life. You can say, for example, that you don't like parties because they are hot and you feel closed in, or that you are shy and don't like meeting new people. Don't unload all of your problems at once on to an unsuspecting or unprepared friend, but if you explain some of your difficulties in a simple way, most people will try to help.

Why some people won't help

Some people won't help because they feel threatened by your problems. They may feel insecure themselves for all sorts of reasons, and they feel uneasy about having to face up to your difficulties because they see their own problems reflected in yours. It may well say more about their own ability to deal with their problems than about their attitude to you. They simply back off, and it can mean the premature end of a friendship.

The other reason why people won't help is that they don't know what to do. They feel embarrassed and inadequate, and don't know what to say. If you want to enlist the help of someone else you have to be very careful. Choose the right person, decide what you are going to say to them and choose the right moment.

Explain your difficulty to them, and tell them exactly what you expect them to do.

You may only want them to understand some possibly strange aspect of your behaviour, something which has occurred because of your anxiety, maybe why you take the stairs instead of the lift. Or you may want them to help you to stick to your programme when you are finding the going rough. You might want them to go with you to the supermarket, or on a shopping trip. Make sure they know what is expected of them, and what they can expect of you. If you find one such helpful person you are lucky. Don't unload too many of your problems on to them, don't ask too much even of a wife or husband. Even the best intentioned person in the world can run out of patience. You live with your problem every day. It is always with you, but be careful that you don't let it make you into a bore.

Professional help

There might come a time when you you need to consider seeking professional help. Your situation doesn't have to be too drastic for that to happen. You might just feel that you aren't making progress fast enough, or that you need support which you can't get elsewhere.

If your situation is getting worse instead of better then you should seek help. If you aren't sleeping, if you are waking early in the morning and if you are feeling sad and tearful then you must see your doctor because you just might be depressed, and that requires different treatment. If you anxiety is making you drink, do something about it, and if it is causing you problems at work or in your marriage you should ask someone for help. You have nothing to lose.

Your doctor

Your doctor is the most accessible professional person you can talk to. You can make an appointment to see him or her anytime, and your doctor will listen to your problems and try to help. I happen to be a family doctor so I know something about this kind of medicine, and I can assure you that people bring all kinds of problems to us, and the most common problems we see are those to do with anxiety and stress. Some surveys suggest that up to 50 per cent of the consultations a family doctor has with patients are for psychological problems.

These problems are of all types. Very often a person suffering from the physical symptoms created by an overactive nervous system assumes that there is something physically wrong with him or with her, and that is not an unreasonable assumption. On other occasions the patient knows that he or she has an anxiety state and simply wants help.

What can you expect from your doctor?

Doctors are very variable in their response to the problems produced by anxiety. They all have experience and training and you might be surprised by how helpful your doctor will be. Someone whom you have thought of as a bit of a fuddy-duddy may show surprising insight born of years of experience.

A doctor may want to do several things. He or she may want to make sure that you don't have a physical illness such as an overactive thyroid gland. If your anxiety is situational then this is unlikely, but he or she may want to check just in case because doctors are trained to look for physical causes for symptoms. The doctor may take a blood test, and give you an overall physical check-up as well.

The doctor may also want to make sure that you aren't depressed, because the treatment of depression is different from the treatment of anxiety and it isn't always that easy to distinguish between the two. Both of them can produce physical symptoms. If you are depressed you might be helped by anti-depressant medication, and there is no real alternative to that. Depression is a self-limiting and curable condition, and will always get better, but if it is serious you will need medical help.

What can your doctor do for you?

Your doctor can help you. He or she might have been of more help if you had not read this book and were starting from scratch because then he or she would have been able to tell you many of the things I have already told you in the book. Now you already know much of what you might be told to you, but you can always discuss your actual, specific, problems and that in itself can be a great help, particularly if you had been thinking that you were the only one who had ever suffered from anxiety. It is a great relief to find out that you have a common, treatable condition rather than some strange and disturbing illness.

If you want to take your problems further there are two options open to your doctor. You can be given medication, or referred to a specialist.

Other professionals

Psychiatrists

There are other professionals who take an interest in anxiety. Everyone knows about psychiatrists. They are the doctors who ask you to lie on a couch and tell them all about your dreams and childhood fantasies, aren't they? Well, not quite. Sigmund Freud invented the twentieth-century discipline of psycho-analysis, in which all psychological problems were blamed on unresolved conflicts, usually of a sexual nature. It was thought that if these conflicts could be brought out into the open, the resulting problems could be resolved.

Unfortunately there is no evidence that psychoanalysis actually cures psychiatric problems. Few psychiatrists in the UK practise that kind of treatment, and certainly not on the National Health Service, although it is very much more commonplace in the US. Psychiatrists tend to be more interested in the 'major' psychiatric illnesses, and those who are interested in the treatment of anxiety states use behavioural techniques such as those I have described. Your GP probably wouldn't refer you to a psychiatrist unless you were suffering from a condition which might at some time require admission to hospital, and that is unlikely in anxiety states.

Psychologists

Psychologists aren't medically-trained doctors. They are university graduates in the science of psychology, and they are the people who over the years have developed the techniques described in this book. There are two branches of clinical psychology, the behavioural branch and the analytical, or Freudian branch. The former involves the study of learned human behaviour, and the latter is the theory of unresolved conflicts. Most psychologists follow the behavioural approach these days because it can be shown to work.

Psychologists used to work in psychiatric units and spent most of their time doing psychological tests (remember the ink-blot test?). Nowadays they are directly involved in treating patients with anxiety states and phobic-type disorders. They often work in the community from health centres, and many GPs can refer you to them for help. They have more time than GPs, and they have specialist training. They may also run group therapy classes. A good clinical psychologist can be the most helpful of all the professionals who are available to you. Anxiety is their subject and they know a great deal about it, and have a lot of experience treating it.

Community psychiatric nurses (CPNs)

Psychiatric nurses don't do the same sort of nursing that general nurses do. There are no surgical wounds to dress, and less in the way of bed pans. In psychiatric hospitals they are involved in the ward treatment programme, and now they have been moved into the community nursing situation, rather like district nurses. They also work from health centres, and will take referrals from GPs. They tend to have time to spend with patients, and use the same general principles as the other professionals we have mentioned.

Your GP may be able to refer you to a CPN. They also run group therapy sessions and can be very helpful.

Physiotherapists

Physiotherapists aren't primarily involved in the treatment of anxiety problems, but they can be helpful in some situations particularly where there has been a loss of confidence. If you have developed difficulty in say, walking, problems crossing the street, or with feelings of imbalance, physiotherapists can use their particular skills to improve your confidence and help to improve your motor control. They are also very good at teaching relaxation and breathing exercises, which they also teach to pregnant women at antenatal classes.

Occupational therapists

Occupational therapists usually work in the hospital service with infirm, convalescent or partially disabled patients, but they have expertise in helping patients to regain their ability and confidence, and occasionally can be helpful to anxious people. They teach particular practical skills.

Self-help groups

Getting in touch with a group of people with similar problems can be one of the best sources of help. There are many such groups around, and there may well be one near you. Your doctor may be able to put you in touch with one, or there may be an advertisement in your library or your Citizen's Advice Bureau may have an address.

These groups will give you support, encouragement and advice, and you will meet people who have overcome problems similar to yours. They will be able to offer you group therapy where you may be able to practise with other people the sort of exercises I have described in this book. You will be able to discuss problems you have in common and find out how others solve them. They will be able to advise you about the books you can buy, and may have speakers or even social events.

Group therapy may be organized by such charitable organizations, or it may be organized by a CPN or a psychologist. As with anything else in life, you get out of group therapy very much what you are prepared to put in. Groups have a personality of their own. Some work very well and are very supportive, and some work much less well. I have sat in on groups where one person hogged the discussion with an endless list of complaints which that individual seemed to think were exclusive to him. Groups are not for people seeking sympathy. They are for people who go along with constructive ideas and a desire to listen to other people's problems and to help, because it is often by helping others that you help yourself.

Some people who are naturally private individuals may not want to get involved in group therapy, but there is no doubt that the right group can give you a lot of support. It's something you should consider, but if you want to try group therapy try to find the right group. A high-flying businessperson might not have too much in common with what he or she thinks is a housewives' group and may feel embarrassed in that situation, and vice versa.

All of the above understand anxiety problems and have special skills which can help. Access to them can be gained through your GP, so there is plenty of professional help available if you want it, and it doesn't involve going off to a mental hospital or being treated as a psychiatric patient. Those days are long past. It may well be that your GP has all the expertise you need, because sometimes all you really require is a detached opinion and impartial advice, or even just a friendly voice to tell you that you are on the right lines.

Other practitioners

There are many other kinds of experts you can consult. They practise Alternative Medicine, and there are many disciplines— too many to list and discuss in detail. Each discipline is different, the qualifications of its practitioners are different and the success of the different approaches to treatment is variable. There are many books written about this subject, and you may also be able to seek advice from friends or relatives.

There is no reason why alternative practitioners could not help you. Be wary of someone who promises an instant cure, or a cure which does not require any input from you. There is no way that someone else can banish your anxiety. That takes effort from you over a long time and I am not aware of any short-cuts. All that anyone can do is to guide you along the paths which you must take yourself. You can get support, advice, help and encouragement, but there is no magic.

Remember that there is a logical explanation for the symptoms which you get, and with thought you can often work out what is going on yourself. Don't be tempted to seek cures for individual symptoms if they are part of a greater affliction, and excessive anxiety is a great affliction. You may indeed be able to get rid of one symptom, but it is quite possible that another will take its place. Find someone who will help you to work on your anxiety as a whole.

How not to seek help

A friend of mine, David, developed a moderately severe anxiety state and came to me informally for help. What happened after that is a good example of how one should *not* seek help for one's problems.

For a start, informal help with any problem is fraught with difficulty. If you are merely discussing problems with a friend that is fine because your friend will not profess any great expertise and you can have an open discussion from which you can both benefit. Catching the ear of a so-called expert at a party leads to advice which is neither detached nor informal. If David had wanted proper advice he would have done better making an appointment to see an expert and taken his advice seriously, but David was a high-flyer and didn't see the need to take the same path which ordinary mortals take.

David did come to see me some time later as I had suggested, and he listened to what I had to say very carefully, but as I was talking to him I had the impression that he wasn't convinced by what I had told him, an impression which was born out in our next discussion. When we met again he told me that he had been to see an acupuncturist who had been excellent, and he was feeling much better. As he was talking to me I had a feeling that his improvement wouldn't last.

Again, unfortunately, I was right. When we next met he had been to a hypnotist and was full of his praises, but I was aware that he had made no contribution himself to solving his problem, and was relying on others including myself. As the weeks and months moved on so did David. He went to different practitioners in a relentless search for a cure, and although he did get some short-term release from his anxiety symptoms, he never gave any one practitioner a chance, and he didn't give himself a chance.

David had a fundamental problem, quite apart from his anxiety. He had his own interpretation of what was happening to him, and he had his own idea of how his body worked and how it should work. He was a born sceptic. He was trained to look for quick answers and quick ready-made results, and he didn't really admit the true nature of his condition because he thought of it as a weakness, and he would not entertain the idea that he might have such a weakness. He wanted someone else to cure him, and he really also wanted some other theory which would explain his symptoms without having to admit that he was suffering from anxiety.

The last time I saw David he had just driven to London to see a practitioner in Harley Street, and was anxious to tell me all about it. What this man was suggesting by way of a cure horrified me as much as it excited my friend. It seemed to me that his quest for a therapist had become more of a preoccupation than his medical condition. He was spending a lot of money, but money can't buy health, and sometimes it can be a hindrance. I often meet people who would be healthier, and certainly happier, if they had less money and more sense.

Almost any one of the people David consulted could have

helped him if he had given them the chance. The more ethical of them told him the truth and offered him an approach to his problem. Of course no one is obliged to accept advice offered, and no practitioner has an exclusive right to the truth about health, but you have to accept that advice is usually offered in good faith, that it represents that practitioner's interpretation of the facts as he or she sees them, and the solutions as he or she sees them. David would have done better if he had found a practitioner with ideas which were acceptable to him, and then given the practitioner a chance to help. *One thing is certain in the treatment of anxiety, there are no short-cuts, and the cure takes effort from the sufferer.*

If you can accept this fact then there is no limit to how far you can go, and if you have common sense and determination you can banish your anxiety using the techniques outlined in this book without reference to any other source of information. The important thing is to have faith in the truth of what has been said, to make a start, and most of all to keep at it. You can only have faith in the advice in this book or anywhere else, if it seems to relate to you, if it strikes some sort of a chord, and most of all if you find that it works for you. When you find this sort of advice stick with it and you will win through.

Medication

In general terms medicines, either orthodox or holistic, have a limited place in the treatment of excessive anxiety. It is much better to rely on yourself than on any form of medication, because your anxiety is something which is with you and part of you in the long term, and it is better not to take medicine in the long term unless it is unavoidable. If you have a serious condition like diabetes or high blood-pressure then your doctor may have to advise you to take tablets for the rest of your life. Most people would feel that was inappropriate in the case of an anxiety state.

Medication is inappropriate for another reason. Excessive anxiety is curable if you go about it the right way. Pills only dampen down its effects. Banishing your anxiety isn't easy, and of course you can't change your personality because you would then become a different person, and you probably wouldn't want to do that. If you tend to be an anxious type of person you may remain an anxious person, but anxiety shouldn't ruin your life, or even interfere with the full and complete enjoyment of your life. You can banish the symptoms of anxiety, and you need no help with that beyond that given in this book. The problems related to curing excessive anxiety are to do with motivation, keeping at it, taking the long-term view and having the courage and faith in yourself required to banish this most distressing problem.

The drug Valium has had a high profile, and most people throw up their hands in horror at its mention. It was widely used in the treatment of anxiety but has recently developed a bad reputation and is now less used because of the problems it causes. It is one of the benzodiazepine group of drugs which are also known as tranquillizers.

Valium was introduced as a treatment of sprains and muscle injuries because of its ability to relax muscles, and it is widely used in the form of an intravenous injection as the first-line emergency treatment of epileptic fits. It's ability to release muscle tension was quickly found useful in the treatment of tension states and anxiety, but it was used as an alternative to the sort of measures described in this book, and it was prescribed in the long term so that eventually a pattern of habituation developed. It is interesting that most sleeping tablets still prescribed are also benzodiazepines, but these have escaped the bad publicity that Valium received, and most doctors have great difficulty dissuading many patients from asking for them.

Perhaps the benzodiazepines don't deserve the bad reputation they have. They are the only drugs I can think of to be criticized for the very efficiency which accounts for their over-use. Patients found them effective and wanted to keep taking them, but like any form of medication, uncontrolled use, over-use and lack of supervision lead to problems. In time they will find their proper place—as a useful form of medication for the short-term treatment of acute anxiety. They are certainly not an alternative to relaxation techniques, desensitization and the rest.

Other forms of medication may be helpful particularly for dealing with specific problems. There are drugs which stop diarrhoea effectively, and that might be useful for some people. Pain-relieving medication can be helpful for people with headaches and other forms of muscle pain, but again one must guard against over-use. It would be more convenient, however, if there was a drug which blocked the action of adrenalin.

There *is* such a drug, but it only blocks some of the actions of adrenalin, and that is just as well because most of the actions of adrenalin are advantageous if not essential, and if our adrenalin was turned off we would suffer by it. That is the problem. Anxiety and its physical effects are natural and normal, and often beneficial, so all an anxious person really wants is to have his adrenalin turned down a bit.

Adrenalin has different effects on different organs depending on the receptors in those organs. The receptors in the heart are mostly Beta (β)-receptors, so the drugs we call β-blockers block these receptors and so block most of the effect of adrenalin on the heart. They stop the heart from speeding up and they control palpitations, but have little effect on other organs. β-blockers are also used for the treatment of high blood-pressure and angina because they regulate the beating of the heart, but if you are anxious and have a rapid heart, or palpitations, or anything connected with the heart, β-blockers may make you more comfortable. They may also reduce some other physical effects of adrenalin, and can be helpful for some sufferers from anxiety who have predominantly physical symptoms.

A patient of mine who had been given a β-blocker as a treatment of angina became involved in a bomb scare in Northern Ireland. He had had to evacuate his hotel in the middle of the night, and the hotel had promptly blown up. I asked him if he had not been terrified, and he said the he hadn't been in the least worried, and that nothing had really worried him since he had started on his new medication. It was a quite unsolicited endorsement of a β-blocker for the treatment of anxiety, in this case natural and understandable anxiety.

Some musicians use β-blockers because it improves their performance under stress, and some snooker players have been known to do the same thing, though the drug is now banned in sport. No drug is the complete answer, but some may help. Medication to relieve pain can be useful if muscle tension or headaches cause you real problems. There is good medication which controls diarrhoea if that is a problem. Your doctor can at least give you this sort of help, but he or she may well be able to do more than that by referring you to another professional.

> **REMEMBER:**
> - Be careful whom you confide in. Some people don't understand.
> - Don't hesitate to seek professional help.
> - Don't look for easy cures or short-cuts.
> - Have faith in your own ability and courage.

Chapter 12

Anxiety and lifestyle

We have been considering the nuts and bolts of anxiety up until now, talking about the way anxiety works and the way symptoms are produced. The techniques we have discussed have been practical and straightforward because this approach has been shown to work. Yet there are other considerations.

The psychological implications

Anxiety is a psychological state, albeit with powerful physical manifestations. A person with an anxiety state in which he or she produces too much adrenalin will usually, though not always, feel anxious, and it isn't a pleasant feeling. It makes one feel insecure and uncertain, and it can be hard to live with uncertainties about oneself and one's abilities. People ask themselves: why am I anxious? Why did it start? Am I responsible for my anxiety in some way? Are my parents responsible in some way, maybe because of the way they brought me up? Is it something to do with the stress I endure at work or at home, or is it just that I can't cope? Perhaps there is something fundamentally wrong with my personality?

These are all questions anxious people ask themselves. When you become anxious you are entering uncharted waters, uncharted for you at least. Everyone thinks that they are the first and only one to be anxious. In fact they are joining a secret army of the afflicted, becoming just another one of the many who suffer torment from increased anxiety. Just the same, the answers to these questions are individual answers. The results of increased anxiety are fairly standard, but just as each person is an individual, so the psychological implications of his or her anxiety are different.

If you are to banish your anxiety you must proceed along the lines suggested in this book. That is the way to take on your symptoms and defeat them, but along the way, and perhaps even after you have rid yourself of your anxiety, these doubts and uncertainties may remain. We have touched on them before, only to put them to one side so that we could concentrate on the techniques which would control our symptoms, but this book would be less than complete if we didn't at least consider the psychological implications of anxiety.

Why me?

I suppose we all wonder 'why me?'. Of all the people in the world why should I suffer from a condition which keeps me back, which stops me enjoying life to the full, which stops me from fulfilling my true potential? Of course there is no answer to these questions. You might suffer from asthma or diabetes or any one of a multitude of distressing, dangerous or even fatal illnesses. An anxiety state isn't a serious or a potentially fatal condition, but it is a major problem for someone who suffers from it, and should be considered in that light. You are fortunate that you don't suffer from an illness like diabetes, but you are not as fortunate as someone who has no illness.

But wait a minute! Who has no illnesses, or no problems? Perhaps you have to be a GP to realize that no one is without some problem at some stage in their lives, often a very secret or personal problem which no one knows about. It might be a marital problem, maybe a sexual problem, or even a financial problem. It would be a mistake to envy anyone because you do not know what torments they may be going through. Settle for your own insecurities and dilemmas.

There is a saying that old age doesn't come by itself, and it is true that the advancing years bring difficulties, one of which may be increased anxiety. When we are young everything is possible. If we have problems we may not appreciate their nature, and anyway we were born to overcome everything put in our way. With increasing age comes a little realism, and it may become clear that we cannot achieve all that we wanted to achieve, or that happiness is more elusive than we thought.

So is success. There may be disappointments and difficulties which we may not be able to face up to. Life is more difficult and more complex than we thought.

Realism

When you have begun to control your anxiety you might want to sit back and take stock. You might wish to seek answers to some of these questions, perhaps just so that you will be able to understand yourself and your condition better, and perhaps in the hope that by understanding you will be able to find help with your problems.

This might mean simply coming to see ourselves as others see us, adopting a realistic view of our personality and our public persona, or it might mean an exploration of our private selves, a coming to terms with our true selves so that we can see what we are really like, what our true expectations are and what our abilities are genuinely like. We all fool ourselves just a bit, but if we believe the lie we sell to the world we are in trouble.

This pursuit of realism is quite different from the Freudian concept of exposing subconscious conflicts. That is an exercise which can last a lifetime and in the end I believe it is self-defeating. The type of understanding you are seeking may be a recognition of the obvious, although the things you are interested in understanding may be obvious to everyone but yourself.

You may be seeking a recognition of some truths which are deep within yourself and which you have avoided for so long that you have forgotten about them. In seeking these truths you aren't seeking a cure for your anxiety state. You know how to go about doing that, and there are no short-cuts. You are seeking a better understanding of yourself in the hope that this understanding might explain why you are anxious, and in the hope that it will help you to cope with your symptoms until you have banished them.

Brian

Brian was a quiet, unassuming young man of twenty-two who was unmarried and who didn't have a steady girlfriend. He lived in a flat in the city during the week, but at weekends he tended to go home to his parents' house in a nearby town.

Brian liked outdoor sports and was a keen hill-walker and skier in the winter, and in the summer he sailed with friends at the local yacht club. He had many friends, but somehow there was no one close to him, and although he seemed to be an outgoing, popular individual he wasn't very happy, and he didn't know why. He was unfulfilled, even though he seemed to have everything with the possible exception of a girlfriend, and this was something he should have been able to remedy for himself.

I first encountered Brian when he developed some unpleasant symptoms. He was having panic attacks on public transport, and he was beginning to find meetings difficult. He consulted me because he wanted something done about these apparently serious symptoms, and as he talked I recognized his problem and was able to offer appropriate advice along the lines already discussed in this book. Brian was an ambitious young man who didn't easily accept the concept of a psychological illness, but he agreed to try the approach I suggested. He did reasonably well, but he kept coming back to me with questions. Why had this problem developed? Would it recur? Was there something fundamentally wrong with his make-up?

It became clear to me that Brian was never going to make the progress he would like to make unless he had some sort of logical explanation for his illness. He simply couldn't accept that he was the sort of person who would develop an anxiety state, whereas I wasn't in the least surprised because he seemed to me to be a rather vulnerable, unconfident young man, his true personality being the obverse of his outer image. I began a series of discussions with Brian which I hoped would lead him to a greater understanding of his own problems.

This understanding would not magically banish Brian's anxiety. His anxiety had developed over many years during which his autonomic nervous system had learned the wrong lessons and this was quite separate from his personality problems, but inevitably they were interrelated in some ways. If he could be more comfortable with himself, more relaxed with himself, then physical relaxation might be easier to achieve. Furthermore, if he could develop some understanding of the way his anxiety state had developed, why he had learned the wrong lessons, he might be able to feel less guilty and confused.

Brian talked about his life, about the things he enjoyed and the things he disliked, and as he did so it became clear to me that he was living something of a lie. He didn't really enjoy the macho outdoor life. He was a rather introspective, quiet man who might have preferred more intellectual pursuits. How had he become so hooked on the outdoor life? That wasn't easy to explain, but it seemed that at one stage in his life he had had several friends who enjoyed the outdoor sporting life and he had become involved through them, and as they had been successful he had modelled his own life in theirs. As far as Brian was concerned there was only one way to conduct his life, even though that may have been the wrong way for him.

I couldn't change Brian's life for him; I couldn't even make suggestions, which he might have resented. All I could do was to let him talk so that he might come to his own conclusions about his life. There is nothing to say that Brian could get rid of his anxiety by simply changing his lifestyle. The lessons his body had learned over the years had to be unlearned using relaxation techniques and the like, but the reasons why he had found life stressful, why he had had so many reversals and why he had become uncomfortable were fairly obvious, and it is possible that if he adapted his life he might avoid difficulties in the future.

Somewhere in the past Brian had taken a wrong turn, and in the uphill struggle which his life eventually became he had had so many personal defeats that his body had learned to react by churning out adrenalin in threatening situations. He had become trapped on the downward spiral. He had to begin the process of re-educating his body, but he could also take a critical look at the way he led his life, and also at the details of his behaviour in difficult situations. He needed to do all of these things if he was to banish his anxiety completely.

Changing your life

It is never right to try to change your life entirely in the hope that that will banish your anxiety. Giving up your job, getting a divorce, emigrating, nothing like that will change the way your body works, so you will continue to be anxious. In the long run some changes might relieve a few of the stresses which cause you to have problems, but deal with your anxiety first, then get on with considering your lifestyle. It would be extremely annoying if you changed your life completely only to find that you were the same anxious person, but in a different situation. Make major decisions only after long and careful deliberation.

Your past

Not everyone has obvious reasons for their anxiety. Many anxious people are happily married and seem to lead perfectly balanced and successful lives. It's as if their anxiety is tacked on to an otherwise perfectly normal personality. They certainly aren't neurotic in the lay sense of that word. They are sensible, wise and sensitive. They may have made the correct choices in the past, and their lives may seem to be unstressed. If you are one of these people you have every right to wonder why you have become anxious, but are you seeing the true picture?

Are there some things in your past which you have forgotten about, or dismissed as being unimportant? We all tend to rewrite our past as we go. It makes it easier for us to live with the less happy moments, but we don't really forget. It's amazing what we can remember with a little prompting, and even sitting down with the intention of remembering as much about an event as possible can lead to the most unexpected recollections.

We have agreed that the constant rehearsal of past problems doesn't help our anxiety, and can even be positively harmful, but that doesn't mean that we shouldn't be honest about our past because that will help us to take a realistic view of our current situation and help with decisions about the future. I find the act of writing something down makes for clarity, and what we are seeking now is an accurate impression of just what we were like at different stages of our lives, the way we would have appeared to other people, and how efficiently we coped with life's problems. It might be interesting to know how our anxiety developed, or if we did make unfortunate decisions in our lives. Self-knowledge is always helpful.

One successful method of looking at how anxiety develops is to take one age, say ten years, and write down a few recollections of specific events which stick in the mind. It might be a birthday party, or a family event such as a wedding or a funeral, or it might be a day at school. Something may have happened which makes it more vivid than other days. Choose several such events and make a few notes about how you felt on that day, what you thought about the people there, how they treated you. Do that for several such events before you move on to your next age, say fifteen years. As you go your recollections may become more accurate and more vivid, and some of your memories will be of events and occasions, or a small incident during such events which was embarrassing, something which you don't enjoy recalling at all.

On now to eighteen, or twenty years, whatever you choose. Make the same few notes, but make them as full and as honest as you can, looking at your successes as well as your failures. For each age write a paragraph about the sort of person you were, because you still are that person. You may be older and wiser, but you are still the summation of all that has gone before. Can you come to any conclusions?

It might be that you will see that your anxiety hasn't come out of the blue. You may have had to work very hard over the years to overcome a temperament which has always made you struggle a bit in certain situations. You might even be able to detect some of the reasons why your personality has developed in the way it has, maybe in the way your parents or your siblings have treated you. More likely you will come to the conclusion that you have always had the personality which you have now, and that in the past you have compensated for it very well on most occasions. You might see that you are a sensitive, aware, caring individual, and the price for this side of your personality may be that you tend to be apprehensive and sometimes even anxious. You might feel that that is a bonus. If the price of being a caring, informed individual is an occasional episode of increased anxiety, that might be a price worth paying. No one would choose to be a shallow boor.

Your present

Screw up all those little pieces of paper you have been writing on and throw them away. The last thing you want to do is to dwell on your past. What about the present? You have been looking very hard at the details of your current problems, but it might be worth standing back a little and trying to take a more objective view of your life as a whole. Just what sort of person are you? Go through the same exercise as you did with your past. Look at a few events and consider your attitude to them, and the way you managed difficulties and how you deal with emotional trauma.

What you might need is a little realism, so that you don't have unreal expectations. If it is to your advantage to be your natural self, you have to know what that self really is with no self-deception. Are you pursuing the right goals? Do you set standards for yourself which are too high? Are you fulfilling your potential, or are you held back by unreal fears? It may be frustration brought on by your lack of confidence which is part of the problem, and knowing that may encourage you to pursue confidence-building exercises.

We can all learn lessons from our lives, but don't overdo it. The answer to your immediate problems is to tackle your anxiety on a day-to-day basis using the techniques already described. More self-knowledge may lead you to conclusions about your own value and worth which will encourage you to work harder, but you can't change your basic personality, you can't be someone else.

Your future

You can be yourself, both now and in the future, and you can be all that you want to be. If you have the determination to persist with the exercises in this book you can fulfil your expectations, but as we are involved in a journey through time we might as well carry on into the future. We have looked at the past, looked at the present, what now about the future? Surely if we have some idea of just what sort of lifestyle we wish to achieve, what sort of person we wish to be, then we have something to work towards, some kind of goal to attain.

You may well just wish to carry on as you are now, but perhaps with a little more success and a little less anguish. That would be fine. You might want to simply get back to what you were like before you became overtly anxious, and that too would be a very acceptable ambition, but why not decide to go one step further, to try to be more confident or more able than you were? Look at your past and see if you have been avoiding situations without being aware that you were doing so. It may not be the New Year, but why not make a resolution that in the future you won't avoid any situation because it makes you anxious? It is time you addressed the secret agenda.

The secret agenda

Everyone who has a tendency to be anxious has a secret undercurrent which runs through their lives. There is a secret thread which runs through every transaction they have with another person, something which limits their activities and causes disquiet in the small hours of the night. It is the constant and ever-present knowledge that they are anxious and that nothing they undertake will be straightforward. So a simple invitation in for coffee has to be considered carefully. How do I feel? Who will be there? Will I be able to cope? Nothing, not the most simple invitation or task, is free from this secret constraint.

This unease is always there, lurking in the background. It makes you hesitant about accepting even the most straight-forward invitation, careful about going out to a football match, going shopping—doing anything requires second thoughts. If you have to go to a lecture you think 'Will I be able to sit near a door? Where are the doors? Is it one of those theatres where the doors are at the front so that if I have to leave I will be seen by everyone?' An invitation out to friends for the evening begs the questions, 'How long will I have to stay? Who else will be there and will I make a fool of myself?'

Sometimes the reason for the unease isn't clear. You just don't know why you are uncomfortable, why you feel apprehensive, why you make excuses, but you find that you do, and it is a form of avoidance behaviour. Whatever the reason, you end up sounding unwilling to go for a cup of coffee, so that you may get the reputation of being antisocial. People may begin to exclude you, and if you are young and needing social contacts so that you can make new friends, this kind of social isolation can be disastrous.

It is also humiliating and frustrating. What your friends and workmates don't realize is that you would love to accept their invitation, and would do almost anything to go along with them, but your anxiety holds you back. That little voice of reticence, which may be totally alien to your normal character and contrary to your wishes, reminds you of all the possible dangers which lurk in any invitation. They are probably completely unreal dangers, but if your subconscious self is really in overdrive, your autonomic nervous system will switch on at even the most casual mention of an invitation for a cup of coffee. You will get all those unwanted symptoms and find yourself muttering your excuses yet again.

The result of all this is that you don't do yourself justice. You seem apologetic, shifty, uncomfortable. You hate that part of yourself which seems to work against you, which holds you back. It makes you miserable, and it is worse because no matter how many resolutions you make, you find that you are still making your apologies, still going home alone, still missing out on the party you would love to go to, still presenting yourself in a bad light. It can seem hopeless.

It isn't hopeless. The answers are all in this book, all the relaxation, all the practice, all the ploys to improve your confidence. You can't force this limiting side of your personality away. You have to accept it, work with it, and slowly overcome it. Most of all you have to learn to accept these invitations and accept the consequences, which might be a little discomfort, a feeling of panic, even a panic attack. You really need the courage not to say no, to accept the invitation whatever it is, and resolve to actually go, and know that you have the resources to deal with any difficulties which might arise.

Of course you can develop a plan of action for the regularly occurring phobic situations, but for those casual invitations, for the everyday apprehension which has become part of your life, if it is reasonable to accept that invitation for a cup of coffee or a drink, give it a try and you might be surprised how well you get on.

The stressful lifestyle

Many people wonder if stress has produced their anxiety. They lead stressful lives, or they have been subject to certain specific stresses in the recent past. Often it is when the stress is past that problems begin.

Margaret

Margaret was a middle-aged lady with a growing family of healthy girls and a loyal husband. She was an able and successful individual who had a well-developed sense of duty. She had stayed at home to look after her children as they grew up, and when her own mother had become infirm she had taken her in and looked after her for several years. The presence of the old lady caused friction in the house from time to time, both between Margaret and her husband, and also between herself and her daughters.

Margaret's mother became more frail, and she began to lose her memory and later to hallucinate, developing all the signs of senile dementia. The problems in the house continued to get worse and eventual her mother couldn't be left alone at all. Holidays were out of the question, and it became difficult to get a night out with her husband. The strains on her marriage began to show.

Then, at an advanced age, Margaret's mother died after a long period of increasing frailty, and it was generally felt that her death was something of a release. Soon after Margaret came to me and told me about the problems she was experiencing in the supermarket. She had begun to feel panicky at the check-out, and at busy times sometimes felt that she might cry out. She had begun to dread the thought of having to go to the supermarket at all. She wanted to know what was happening to her, why it was happening, and what she could do about it.

There could be little doubt that Margaret's problems were related to the stress she had been experiencing, and it was entirely typical that they developed just after that stress had been removed. Her mother's death had been a release even though she had grieved, but it had opened the floodgates of her anxiety. It was almost as if her adrenalin had been used up whilst the stress had been present, but when it was removed that adrenalin was still running at a high level and it was channelled into an anxiety state, and that is often the way anxiety states begin.

So stress can produce an anxiety state just as it can produce, or certainly make worse, many conditions from peptic ulcers to psoriasis. Stress is a potent producer of illness of all sorts, but conversely, anxiety can produce stress if it interferes with work or family. Stress and anxiety chase each other's tails. Stress is just one of the factors which makes anxiety worse, or it can be the withdrawal of stress as in Margaret's case. It is a very complicated inter-relationship. But stress is part of our lives. Many people thrive on a stressful lifestyle and simply wouldn't be happy leading a quiet life in the country. They may become actors or mountain climbers or deep sea divers, and people such as these are just as likely to have the symptoms or the illnesses produced by stress as the rest of us, but accept them or even welcome them as part of their feeling of fulfilment.

Other people have to lead stressful lifestyles out of necessity. They may begin a job and later find that there are personality problems operating in their place of work which produce severe stress, or their sales manager may require higher and higher sales figures, or there may be the threat of redundancy. Then there are problems with illness or difficulties in a marriage, or all sorts of seemingly minor things which build up over the years. Stress can be very subtle, and often its first manifestation will be physical symptoms, and these can be corrosive and even disabling, but they may not be as serious as they can first seem.

If stress produces an illness such as a duodenal ulcer, or if it contributes to your high blood-pressure or even to a heart attack, this is serious. You can do nothing about it. If stress produces an anxiety state you are lucky, because anxiety is just an exaggeration of your normal physiology and in itself it can do you no harm. Extensive research has shown that it will not shorten your life, though of course it may affect your life by making it difficult for you to pursue your occupation or lead a normal, comfortable existence. It can cause you real problems if you let it, but unlike some other medical conditions you can do something about it. Anxiety is eminently treatable, and you can treat it yourself without help from anyone else if you wish.

Your personality

All sorts of people develop excessive anxiety, but in my experience most people who do so are nice people. That's a very subjective judgment, but there may be an element of truth in it. Brash, loud-mouthed, uncaring people aren't likely to develop anxiety states, are they? Such people never have self-doubts. Gentle, caring, involved, sensitive people may become anxious as they react to the changes in their lives. They can see the other person's point of view, empathize with others in trouble and share the cares of the world. Anxious people may be ambitious and driving, may be achievers who reach the heights of their profession and enjoy great success. It is concern for others which produces anxiety, worries about how they feel and what they think about you. If you genuinely don't care what others feel or think, you won't become anxious.

Anxiety may be the price you pay for being a caring person, because if caring is an element of your personality you are vulnerable to anxiety. It is nothing to be ashamed of. All sorts of people do become anxious, but it is the element of humanity which makes so many people of all personality types experience excessive anxiety. It is there to test you, because your experiences of life have educated your body as well as informing your mind, and as you have learned compassion your body has learned to produce adrenalin. In some ways compassion and humanity are alien to the hardness of nature, with all its cruelties and viciousness. Anxiety may be the price you pay, but it may be a price worth paying. You must be the judge of that.

REMEMBER:

- Stress can produce anxiety.
- Sometimes the withdrawal of a particular stress can bring on anxiety.
- Anxiety itself can be stressful.
- Compassionate people are vulnerable to anxiety.
- Anxiety won't shorten your life. Unlike many other stress-related illnesses, anxiety can be cured.

Conclusion

What next?

We have started down the road to recovery. What lies in store? Discovering that you have what we have called an anxiety state is a frightening experience. For the first time you discover that you aren't totally in control of your body. You have now started to regain that control, but will the spectre of a return of your anxiety state follow you for the rest of your life? And why did it happen in the first place?

Your attitudes

It helps if you can take a positive attitude to your anxiety. Some people fear that they will be defeated by their anxiety, that ultimately they will not be able to banish it. Defeat is an emotional word. It implies failure, some kind of shortcoming on their part, an inability to cope. They are somehow less able than other people, and as a result less worthy. You might even feel these things about yourself from time to time, but are they true? The answer is a definite no.

Anxious people come in all shapes and sizes. They are from all walks of life, all social strata, they are both men and women. They have all sorts of different personalities, but they do have one thing in common. In my experience, they are all courageous, they want to get well, and they are copers despite their difficulties. It may be that most ordinary people have the capacity to be courageous but they have little opportunity to demonstrate their courage, whilst the anxious person has to demonstrate it every day.

The stereotype of the anxious person as a neurotic housewife, or the office wimp, is far removed from the truth. An anxiety state is medically classified as a neurosis, but in the clinical rather than the lay sense of that word. Neurosis really means a minor psychological disorder, but we know that it can have major consequences. By and large we face up to them without too much complaint.

So it is now time, after all the discussion, all the explanation, all the advice, to take a good look at ourselves. We aren't defeated. We aren't less worthy than anyone else, and we probably cope better than most. We may be worn down by the constant symptoms of anxiety, but we have now turned the corner. The only way is up. Let's take a look at ourselves.

Let's literally do that. Why don't you stand in front of the mirror and take stock in the light of all that's been said. Exactly who are you? Are you any less of a person than the other people at your place of work? Are you less able? Do you look any less competent? Is there really anything to distinguish you from anyone else you are likely to meet? Deep down you know that you are someone of substance, and that many other people aren't. For many years you have been selling yourself short.

That idea isn't much use to you whilst you are standing in front of your bedroom mirror. If you really feel that you are the equal of anyone, why don't you make practical use of it? You have the tools which will allow you to do more and more, to be more and more comfortable, but you still have to convince yourself that you are just as able as anyone else. The way that I have suggested that you do this is to actually prove it to yourself, and also to your own body, which is responsible for the symptoms you get. You can only do that by actually doing the things which you think you can't do, by surviving them and perhaps even enjoying them. But don't just stop there.

Allow yourself a little self-indulgence. Allow yourself to feel good, to be just a little arrogant. When you go into a room, when you meet someone new, know that you are as good as anyone else and better than most. That is a value judgement, but you must value yourself first if anyone else is to value you.

If you still have trouble doing this, ask yourself why. We have agreed that there is little to be gained by rehearsing your past life looking for hidden emotional conflicts, but taking a realistic look at the way you feel or have felt in individual situations is quite different. I remember once making a fool of myself during a meeting with an eminent professor simply because I felt overawed and inferior. Later I heard him speak at the conference and he was terrible. He made numerous errors of fact and was torn to pieces during the subsequent question time. I was furious with myself for wasting so much emotion, and for appearing so inept. I had no reason to be overawed and resolved not to be in a similar situation in the future. It was something to build on.

Maybe you could try to think a little more positively. When you are in a difficult situation use your relaxation techniques and the rest of what you have learned from this book, but also ask yourself what is going on. What are the dynamics of the situation? Is the person that you feel is threatening to you a bully to everyone else as well? Is your presentation at a meeting as good as anyone else's, and if so shouldn't you be justifiably proud of it and if necessary say so?

By all means wonder if it is hot and if you are sweating, and if that's why you are feeling panicky. That's first aid stuff, but when you get home, wonder what it is in the past which might have made you feel phobic in that situation. I don't mean that you are going to find great Freudian revelations, but do seek some kind of reason, some kind of logic which will make the thing more understandable and so more bearable. Do a little thinking along with your relaxation, and make sure that it is good, positive thinking.

Acceptance

You have to keep nibbling away at your anxiety state from whatever angle you can. Thinking through difficult situations is one way, but you can't change what you think about. You can rationalize things, sort them out in your mind, but it may be that at the end of the day you realize that you have thoughts and ideas which seem simply irrational. There is always some sort of logic to phobias, but it can be a long and tenuous connection between that logic and the problems you get with any given situation. What can you do then?

One thing which might help is just accepting the way you feel and accepting the thoughts which you might have. This isn't a defeatist attitude. It doesn't mean giving up. I am talking about positive acceptance, realizing that you can't change the things that you think about or expel the thoughts which come into your head. Fighting to control your thoughts will simply pump up your adrenalin and make things worse.

Let's say that you have the fixed feeling that you might make a fool of yourself in a public place by shouting out or something like that. If you know that you tend to have that feeling, accept it, expect it and let it wash over you when you think it. Concentrate instead on your relaxation and your breathing, but not to the extent that you are desperately using your exercises to force unwelcome thoughts or ideas away. Logic and your experience tells you that the things you fear don't happen, so believe in your logic and in yourself.

Accept also that some situations will continue to be difficult in the short term. If you can manage to be a little laid-back it helps because you know that in the long term things will come right. You can't force things to happen. Everything in this book has been about relaxing, practising, slowing down and letting things happen. And they will happen: slowly, like a photograph developing, the cloudiness clears and you can see your world a little better and manage it a little better.

Keeping at it

Of all the things which have been said in this book, perhaps this paragraph says the most important. Your progress will be slow, and if you are to succeed in banishing your anxiety, you must actually do the exercises described and *you must keep at it!*

All the advice is quite simple, deceptively so. It may seem straightforward, but it is more difficult to make progress than you might expect. I compared it in a previous chapter to trying to lose weight. All you have to do is eat less, yet there is an entire industry devoted to dieting, hundreds of books, videos, TV programmes, you name it—all about losing weight. Eating less is the most difficult thing in the world to do. Some people can do it in the short term, but that's no good. You have to develop eating habits which will last you all of your life.

I am talking about developing lasting habits of relaxation because you certainly don't want to pass this way again. It isn't as difficult as trying to lose weight, but it does take determination and you have to stick at it even when progress is disappointingly slow. There is nothing easy about that. If you can persuade someone to help you that might make a difference. If you can keep a diary that will help because you can look back to what things were like before, maybe six months previously. You might still not feel too comfortable, but you might notice that you are doing more, going to more places and perhaps enjoying life more. Mark that down as progress.

You must, must, keep at it. Devise your own exercises, look at your own life critically, do your own thing if it helps you, but you owe it to yourself to keep working at your problem from whatever angle you can because one thing I promise you, you can reduce your anxiety, you can lead a fuller, happier, more fulfilled life, and if you really want to, you can banish your anxiety.

Your future

Your future is better than your past. Everyone can improve his or her situation, but you can do better than that. You can banish your anxiety. The facts are these. The dividing line between anxiety which is just annoying, the sort of anxiety which everyone experiences, and anxiety which is in some way disabling, is a very fine one. We all have the potential for crossing over it in either direction. That's why your non-anxious friends feel so vulnerable. They know that they can slide over the line. A tiny reduction in your level of anxiety can shift you across that line in the other direction. When you cross the line you might still feel anxious, but you will be able to cope and you will be in charge of your autonomic nervous system rather than having it in charge of you.

If you are just a little anxious, crossing that line doesn't take a huge effort. If you are just concerned about your year as club chairman, the exercises in this book will help you to cope. If on the other hand, you have been anxious and increasingly demoralized over many years, you have further to go. You should make the effort. There is no reason why you should live a life which is second best. You must be all that you can be, and the good thing is that it is possible to do that.

Everyone, no matter how bad their anxiety, no matter how long they have been anxious, can banish their anxiety. The worse your anxiety is, the more you have to gain, the more incentive you have to work at your problem, and the more progress you can make.

I hope that now your cloud has a silver lining. I hope that you can see a way forward, a way of approaching your problem which has a simple logic, and which I promise you gives results. If you have been in a long tunnel at the end of which there has been no light, I believe that we have lit a candle of hope. You must go forward. You must believe that you can banish your anxiety for one reason—believe it because it is true.

You see, it may be a closely guarded secret, but you aren't the only anxious person in the world, and many people in your situation have banished their anxiety. There is a community of people who know exactly how you feel, who have been there before, and who would wish you to strive and to succeed as they have done. Join that community who have crossed the line into a more comfortable, more fulfilled and less anxious life.

May I wish you every success.

Index